DEAR FUTURE EXAM SUCCESS STORY

First of all, **THANK YOU** for purchasing Mometrix study materials!

Second, congratulations! You are one of the few determined test-takers who are committed to doing whatever it takes to excel on your exam. **You have come to the right place.** We developed these study materials with one goal in mind: to deliver you the information you need in a format that's concise and easy to use.

In addition to optimizing your guide for the content of the test, we've outlined our recommended steps for breaking down the preparation process into small, attainable goals so you can make sure you stay on track.

We've also analyzed the entire test-taking process, identifying the most common pitfalls and showing how you can overcome them and be ready for any curveball the test throws you.

Standardized testing is one of the biggest obstacles on your road to success, which only increases the importance of doing well in the high-pressure, high-stakes environment of test day. Your results on this test could have a significant impact on your future, and this guide provides the information and practical advice to help you achieve your full potential on test day.

Your success is our success

We would love to hear from you! If you would like to share the story of your exam success or if you have any questions or comments in regard to our products, please contact us at **800-673-8175** or **support@mometrix.com**.

Thanks again for your business and we wish you continued success!

Sincerely,
The Mometrix Test Preparation Team

Need more help? Check out our flashcards at:
http://mometrixflashcards.com/NYSTCE

Written and edited by the Mometrix Exam Secrets Test Prep Team
Printed in the United States of America

Mometrix
TEST PREPARATION

NYSTCE®
Theater (166)
Secrets Study Guide

TABLE OF CONTENTS

Introduction

Thank you for purchasing this resource! You have made the choice to prepare yourself for a test that could have a huge impact on your future, and this guide is designed to help you be fully ready for test day. Obviously, it's important to have a solid understanding of the test material, but you also need to be prepared for the unique environment and stressors of the test, so that you can perform to the best of your abilities.

For this purpose, the first section that appears in this guide is the **Secret Keys**. We've devoted countless hours to meticulously researching what works and what doesn't, and we've boiled down our findings to the five most impactful steps you can take to improve your performance on the test. We start at the beginning with study planning and move through the preparation process, all the way to the testing strategies that will help you get the most out of what you know when you're finally sitting in front of the test.

We recommend that you start preparing for your test as far in advance as possible. However, if you've bought this guide as a last-minute study resource and only have a few days before your test, we recommend that you skip over the first two Secret Keys since they address a long-term study plan.

If you struggle with **test anxiety**, we strongly encourage you to check out our recommendations for how you can overcome it. Test anxiety is a formidable foe, but it can be beaten, and we want to make sure you have the tools you need to defeat it.

Secret Key #1 – Plan Big, Study Small

There's a lot riding on your performance. If you want to ace this test, you're going to need to keep your skills sharp and the material fresh in your mind. You need a plan that lets you review everything you need to know while still fitting in your schedule. We'll break this strategy down into three categories.

Information Organization

Start with the information you already have: the official test outline. From this, you can make a complete list of all the concepts you need to cover before the test. Organize these concepts into groups that can be studied together, and create a list of any related vocabulary you need to learn so you can brush up on any difficult terms. You'll want to keep this vocabulary list handy once you actually start studying since you may need to add to it along the way.

Time Management

Once you have your set of study concepts, decide how to spread them out over the time you have left before the test. Break your study plan into small, clear goals so you have a manageable task for each day and know exactly what you're doing. Then just focus on one small step at a time. When you manage your time this way, you don't need to spend hours at a time studying. Studying a small block of content for a short period each day helps you retain information better and avoid stressing over how much you have left to do. You can relax knowing that you have a plan to cover everything in time. In order for this strategy to be effective though, you have to start studying early and stick to your schedule. Avoid the exhaustion and futility that comes from last-minute cramming!

Study Environment

The environment you study in has a big impact on your learning. Studying in a coffee shop, while probably more enjoyable, is not likely to be as fruitful as studying in a quiet room. It's important to keep distractions to a minimum. You're only planning to study for a short block of time, so make the most of it. Don't pause to check your phone or get up to find a snack. It's also important to **avoid multitasking**. Research has consistently shown that multitasking will make your studying dramatically less effective. Your study area should also be comfortable and well-lit so you don't have the distraction of straining your eyes or sitting on an uncomfortable chair.

The time of day you study is also important. You want to be rested and alert. Don't wait until just before bedtime. Study when you'll be most likely to comprehend and remember. Even better, if you know what time of day your test will be, set that time aside for study. That way your brain will be used to working on that subject at that specific time and you'll have a better chance of recalling information.

Finally, it can be helpful to team up with others who are studying for the same test. Your actual studying should be done in as isolated an environment as possible, but the work of organizing the information and setting up the study plan can be divided up. In between study sessions, you can discuss with your teammates the concepts that you're all studying and quiz each other on the details. Just be sure that your teammates are as serious about the test as you are. If you find that your study time is being replaced with social time, you might need to find a new team.

Secret Key #2 – Make Your Studying Count

You're devoting a lot of time and effort to preparing for this test, so you want to be absolutely certain it will pay off. This means doing more than just reading the content and hoping you can remember it on test day. It's important to make every minute of study count. There are two main areas you can focus on to make your studying count.

Retention

It doesn't matter how much time you study if you can't remember the material. You need to make sure you are retaining the concepts. To check your retention of the information you're learning, try recalling it at later times with minimal prompting. Try carrying around flashcards and glance at one or two from time to time or ask a friend who's also studying for the test to quiz you.

To enhance your retention, look for ways to put the information into practice so that you can apply it rather than simply recalling it. If you're using the information in practical ways, it will be much easier to remember. Similarly, it helps to solidify a concept in your mind if you're not only reading it to yourself but also explaining it to someone else. Ask a friend to let you teach them about a concept you're a little shaky on (or speak aloud to an imaginary audience if necessary). As you try to summarize, define, give examples, and answer your friend's questions, you'll understand the concepts better and they will stay with you longer. Finally, step back for a big picture view and ask yourself how each piece of information fits with the whole subject. When you link the different concepts together and see them working together as a whole, it's easier to remember the individual components.

Finally, practice showing your work on any multi-step problems, even if you're just studying. Writing out each step you take to solve a problem will help solidify the process in your mind, and you'll be more likely to remember it during the test.

Modality

Modality simply refers to the means or method by which you study. Choosing a study modality that fits your own individual learning style is crucial. No two people learn best in exactly the same way, so it's important to know your strengths and use them to your advantage.

For example, if you learn best by visualization, focus on visualizing a concept in your mind and draw an image or a diagram. Try color-coding your notes, illustrating them, or creating symbols that will trigger your mind to recall a learned concept. If you learn best by hearing or discussing information, find a study partner who learns the same way or read aloud to yourself. Think about how to put the information in your own words. Imagine that you are giving a lecture on the topic and record yourself so you can listen to it later.

For any learning style, flashcards can be helpful. Organize the information so you can take advantage of spare moments to review. Underline key words or phrases. Use different colors for different categories. Mnemonic devices (such as creating a short list in which every item starts with the same letter) can also help with retention. Find what works best for you and use it to store the information in your mind most effectively and easily.

Secret Key #3 – Practice the Right Way

Your success on test day depends not only on how many hours you put into preparing, but also on whether you prepared the right way. It's good to check along the way to see if your studying is paying off. One of the most effective ways to do this is by taking practice tests to evaluate your progress. Practice tests are useful because they show exactly where you need to improve. Every time you take a practice test, pay special attention to these three groups of questions:

- The questions you got wrong
- The questions you had to guess on, even if you guessed right
- The questions you found difficult or slow to work through

This will show you exactly what your weak areas are, and where you need to devote more study time. Ask yourself why each of these questions gave you trouble. Was it because you didn't understand the material? Was it because you didn't remember the vocabulary? Do you need more repetitions on this type of question to build speed and confidence? Dig into those questions and figure out how you can strengthen your weak areas as you go back to review the material.

Additionally, many practice tests have a section explaining the answer choices. It can be tempting to read the explanation and think that you now have a good understanding of the concept. However, an explanation likely only covers part of the question's broader context. Even if the explanation makes perfect sense, **go back and investigate** every concept related to the question until you're positive you have a thorough understanding.

As you go along, keep in mind that the practice test is just that: practice. Memorizing these questions and answers will not be very helpful on the actual test because it is unlikely to have any of the same exact questions. If you only know the right answers to the sample questions, you won't be prepared for the real thing. **Study the concepts** until you understand them fully, and then you'll be able to answer any question that shows up on the test.

It's important to wait on the practice tests until you're ready. If you take a test on your first day of study, you may be overwhelmed by the amount of material covered and how much you need to learn. Work up to it gradually.

On test day, you'll need to be prepared for answering questions, managing your time, and using the test-taking strategies you've learned. It's a lot to balance, like a mental marathon that will have a big impact on your future. Like training for a marathon, you'll need to start slowly and work your way up. When test day arrives, you'll be ready.

Start with the strategies you've read in the first two Secret Keys—plan your course and study in the way that works best for you. If you have time, consider using multiple study resources to get different approaches to the same concepts. It can be helpful to see difficult concepts from more than one angle. Then find a good source for practice tests. Many times, the test website will suggest potential study resources or provide sample tests.

Practice Test Strategy

If you're able to find at least three practice tests, we recommend this strategy:

Untimed and Open-Book Practice

Take the first test with no time constraints and with your notes and study guide handy. Take your time and focus on applying the strategies you've learned.

Timed and Open-Book Practice

Take the second practice test open-book as well, but set a timer and practice pacing yourself to finish in time.

Timed and Closed-Book Practice

Take any other practice tests as if it were test day. Set a timer and put away your study materials. Sit at a table or desk in a quiet room, imagine yourself at the testing center, and answer questions as quickly and accurately as possible.

Keep repeating timed and closed-book tests on a regular basis until you run out of practice tests or it's time for the actual test. Your mind will be ready for the schedule and stress of test day, and you'll be able to focus on recalling the material you've learned.

Secret Key #4 – Pace Yourself

Once you're fully prepared for the material on the test, your biggest challenge on test day will be managing your time. Just knowing that the clock is ticking can make you panic even if you have plenty of time left. Work on pacing yourself so you can build confidence against the time constraints of the exam. Pacing is a difficult skill to master, especially in a high-pressure environment, so **practice is vital**.

Set time expectations for your pace based on how much time is available. For example, if a section has 60 questions and the time limit is 30 minutes, you know you have to average 30 seconds or less per question in order to answer them all. Although 30 seconds is the hard limit, set 25 seconds per question as your goal, so you reserve extra time to spend on harder questions. When you budget extra time for the harder questions, you no longer have any reason to stress when those questions take longer to answer.

Don't let this time expectation distract you from working through the test at a calm, steady pace, but keep it in mind so you don't spend too much time on any one question. Recognize that taking extra time on one question you don't understand may keep you from answering two that you do understand later in the test. If your time limit for a question is up and you're still not sure of the answer, mark it and move on, and come back to it later if the time and the test format allow. If the testing format doesn't allow you to return to earlier questions, just make an educated guess; then put it out of your mind and move on.

On the easier questions, be careful not to rush. It may seem wise to hurry through them so you have more time for the challenging ones, but it's not worth missing one if you know the concept and just didn't take the time to read the question fully. Work efficiently but make sure you understand the question and have looked at all of the answer choices, since more than one may seem right at first.

Even if you're paying attention to the time, you may find yourself a little behind at some point. You should speed up to get back on track, but do so wisely. Don't panic; just take a few seconds less on each question until you're caught up. Don't guess without thinking, but do look through the answer choices and eliminate any you know are wrong. If you can get down to two choices, it is often worthwhile to guess from those. Once you've chosen an answer, move on and don't dwell on any that you skipped or had to hurry through. If a question was taking too long, chances are it was one of the harder ones, so you weren't as likely to get it right anyway.

On the other hand, if you find yourself getting ahead of schedule, it may be beneficial to slow down a little. The more quickly you work, the more likely you are to make a careless mistake that will affect your score. You've budgeted time for each question, so don't be afraid to spend that time. Practice an efficient but careful pace to get the most out of the time you have.

Secret Key #5 – Have a Plan for Guessing

When you're taking the test, you may find yourself stuck on a question. Some of the answer choices seem better than others, but you don't see the one answer choice that is obviously correct. What do you do?

The scenario described above is very common, yet most test takers have not effectively prepared for it. Developing and practicing a plan for guessing may be one of the single most effective uses of your time as you get ready for the exam.

In developing your plan for guessing, there are three questions to address:

- When should you start the guessing process?
- How should you narrow down the choices?
- Which answer should you choose?

When to Start the Guessing Process

Unless your plan for guessing is to select C every time (which, despite its merits, is not what we recommend), you need to leave yourself enough time to apply your answer elimination strategies. Since you have a limited amount of time for each question, that means that if you're going to give yourself the best shot at guessing correctly, you have to decide quickly whether or not you will guess.

Of course, the best-case scenario is that you don't have to guess at all, so first, see if you can answer the question based on your knowledge of the subject and basic reasoning skills. Focus on the key words in the question and try to jog your memory of related topics. Give yourself a chance to bring the knowledge to mind, but once you realize that you don't have (or you can't access) the knowledge you need to answer the question, it's time to start the guessing process.

It's almost always better to start the guessing process too early than too late. It only takes a few seconds to remember something and answer the question from knowledge. Carefully eliminating wrong answer choices takes longer. Plus, going through the process of eliminating answer choices can actually help jog your memory.

Summary: Start the guessing process as soon as you decide that you can't answer the question based on your knowledge.

How to Narrow Down the Choices

The next chapter in this book (**Test-Taking Strategies**) includes a wide range of strategies for how to approach questions and how to look for answer choices to eliminate. You will definitely want to read those carefully, practice them, and figure out which ones work best for you. Here though, we're going to address a mindset rather than a particular strategy.

Your odds of guessing an answer correctly depend on how many options you are choosing from.

Number of options left	5	4	3	2	1
Odds of guessing correctly	20%	25%	33%	50%	100%

You can see from this chart just how valuable it is to be able to eliminate incorrect answers and make an educated guess, but there are two things that many test takers do that cause them to miss out on the benefits of guessing:

- Accidentally eliminating the correct answer
- Selecting an answer based on an impression

We'll look at the first one here, and the second one in the next section.

To avoid accidentally eliminating the correct answer, we recommend a thought exercise called **the $5 challenge**. In this challenge, you only eliminate an answer choice from contention if you are willing to bet $5 on it being wrong. Why $5? Five dollars is a small but not insignificant amount of money. It's an amount you could afford to lose but wouldn't want to throw away. And while losing $5 once might not hurt too much, doing it twenty times will set you back $100. In the same way, each small decision you make—eliminating a choice here, guessing on a question there—won't by itself impact your score very much, but when you put them all together, they can make a big difference. By holding each answer choice elimination decision to a higher standard, you can reduce the risk of accidentally eliminating the correct answer.

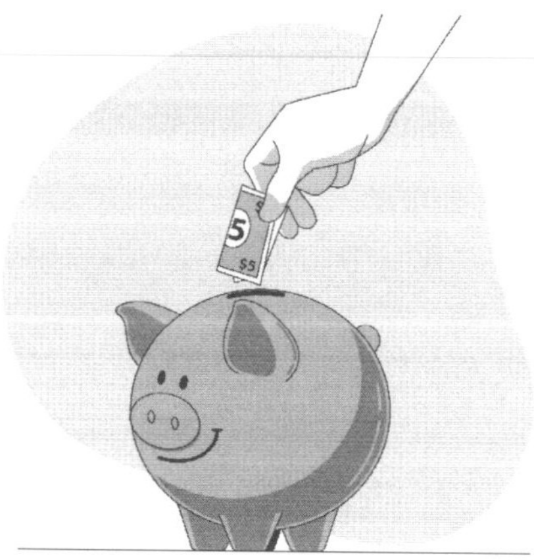

The $5 challenge can also be applied in a positive sense: If you are willing to bet $5 that an answer choice *is* correct, go ahead and mark it as correct.

Summary: Only eliminate an answer choice if you are willing to bet $5 that it is wrong.

Which Answer to Choose

You're taking the test. You've run into a hard question and decided you'll have to guess. You've eliminated all the answer choices you're willing to bet $5 on. Now you have to pick an answer. Why do we even need to talk about this? Why can't you just pick whichever one you feel like when the time comes?

The answer to these questions is that if you don't come into the test with a plan, you'll rely on your impression to select an answer choice, and if you do that, you risk falling into a trap. The test writers know that everyone who takes their test will be guessing on some of the questions, so they intentionally write wrong answer choices to seem plausible. You still have to pick an answer though, and if the wrong answer choices are designed to look right, how can you ever be sure that you're not falling for their trap? The best solution we've found to this dilemma is to take the decision out of your hands entirely. Here is the process we recommend:

Once you've eliminated any choices that you are confident (willing to bet $5) are wrong, select the first remaining choice as your answer.

Whether you choose to select the first remaining choice, the second, or the last, the important thing is that you use some preselected standard. Using this approach guarantees that you will not be enticed into selecting an answer choice that looks right, because you are not basing your decision on how the answer choices look.

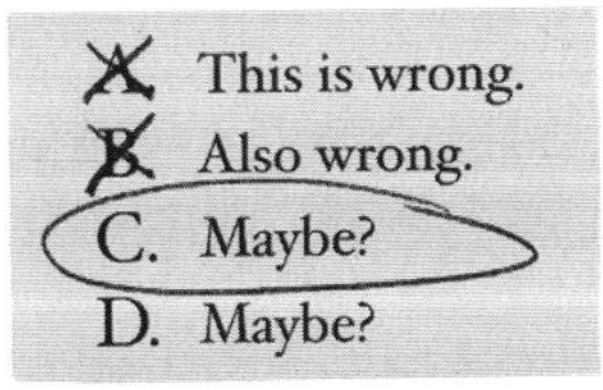

This is not meant to make you question your knowledge. Instead, it is to help you recognize the difference between your knowledge and your impressions. There's a huge difference between thinking an answer is right because of what you know, and thinking an answer is right because it looks or sounds like it should be right.

Summary: To ensure that your selection is appropriately random, make a predetermined selection from among all answer choices you have not eliminated.

Test-Taking Strategies

This section contains a list of test-taking strategies that you may find helpful as you work through the test. By taking what you know and applying logical thought, you can maximize your chances of answering any question correctly!

It is very important to realize that every question is different and every person is different: no single strategy will work on every question, and no single strategy will work for every person. That's why we've included all of them here, so you can try them out and determine which ones work best for different types of questions and which ones work best for you.

Question Strategies

☑ Read Carefully

Read the question and the answer choices carefully. Don't miss the question because you misread the terms. You have plenty of time to read each question thoroughly and make sure you understand what is being asked. Yet a happy medium must be attained, so don't waste too much time. You must read carefully and efficiently.

☑ Contextual Clues

Look for contextual clues. If the question includes a word you are not familiar with, look at the immediate context for some indication of what the word might mean. Contextual clues can often give you all the information you need to decipher the meaning of an unfamiliar word. Even if you can't determine the meaning, you may be able to narrow down the possibilities enough to make a solid guess at the answer to the question.

☑ Prefixes

If you're having trouble with a word in the question or answer choices, try dissecting it. Take advantage of every clue that the word might include. Prefixes can be a huge help. Usually, they allow you to determine a basic meaning. *Pre-* means before, *post-* means after, *pro-* is positive, *de-* is negative. From prefixes, you can get an idea of the general meaning of the word and try to put it into context.

☑ Hedge Words

Watch out for critical hedge words, such as *likely, may, can, often, almost, mostly, usually, generally, rarely,* and *sometimes.* Question writers insert these hedge phrases to cover every possibility. Often an answer choice will be wrong simply because it leaves no room for exception. Be on guard for answer choices that have definitive words such as *exactly* and *always.*

☑ Switchback Words

Stay alert for *switchbacks.* These are the words and phrases frequently used to alert you to shifts in thought. The most common switchback words are *but, although,* and *however.* Others include *nevertheless, on the other hand, even though, while, in spite of, despite,* and *regardless of.* Switchback words are important to catch because they can change the direction of the question or an answer choice.

✓ Face Value

When in doubt, use common sense. Accept the situation in the problem at face value. Don't read too much into it. These problems will not require you to make wild assumptions. If you have to go beyond creativity and warp time or space in order to have an answer choice fit the question, then you should move on and consider the other answer choices. These are normal problems rooted in reality. The applicable relationship or explanation may not be readily apparent, but it is there for you to figure out. Use your common sense to interpret anything that isn't clear.

Answer Choice Strategies

✓ Answer Selection

The most thorough way to pick an answer choice is to identify and eliminate wrong answers until only one is left, then confirm it is the correct answer. Sometimes an answer choice may immediately seem right, but be careful. The test writers will usually put more than one reasonable answer choice on each question, so take a second to read all of them and make sure that the other choices are not equally obvious. As long as you have time left, it is better to read every answer choice than to pick the first one that looks right without checking the others.

✓ Answer Choice Families

An answer choice family consists of two (in rare cases, three) answer choices that are very similar in construction and cannot all be true at the same time. If you see two answer choices that are direct opposites or parallels, one of them is usually the correct answer. For instance, if one answer choice says that quantity *x* increases and another either says that quantity *x* decreases (opposite) or says that quantity *y* increases (parallel), then those answer choices would fall into the same family. An answer choice that doesn't match the construction of the answer choice family is more likely to be incorrect. Most questions will not have answer choice families, but when they do appear, you should be prepared to recognize them.

✓ Eliminate Answers

Eliminate answer choices as soon as you realize they are wrong, but make sure you consider all possibilities. If you are eliminating answer choices and realize that the last one you are left with is also wrong, don't panic. Start over and consider each choice again. There may be something you missed the first time that you will realize on the second pass.

✓ Avoid Fact Traps

Don't be distracted by an answer choice that is factually true but doesn't answer the question. You are looking for the choice that answers the question. Stay focused on what the question is asking for so you don't accidentally pick an answer that is true but incorrect. Always go back to the question and make sure the answer choice you've selected actually answers the question and is not merely a true statement.

✓ Extreme Statements

In general, you should avoid answers that put forth extreme actions as standard practice or proclaim controversial ideas as established fact. An answer choice that states the "process should be used in certain situations, if..." is much more likely to be correct than one that states the "process should be discontinued completely." The first is a calm rational statement and doesn't even make a definitive, uncompromising stance, using a hedge word *if* to provide wiggle room, whereas the second choice is far more extreme.

⊘ Benchmark

As you read through the answer choices and you come across one that seems to answer the question well, mentally select that answer choice. This is not your final answer, but it's the one that will help you evaluate the other answer choices. The one that you selected is your benchmark or standard for judging each of the other answer choices. Every other answer choice must be compared to your benchmark. That choice is correct until proven otherwise by another answer choice beating it. If you find a better answer, then that one becomes your new benchmark. Once you've decided that no other choice answers the question as well as your benchmark, you have your final answer.

⊘ Predict the Answer

Before you even start looking at the answer choices, it is often best to try to predict the answer. When you come up with the answer on your own, it is easier to avoid distractions and traps because you will know exactly what to look for. The right answer choice is unlikely to be word-for-word what you came up with, but it should be a close match. Even if you are confident that you have the right answer, you should still take the time to read each option before moving on.

General Strategies

⊘ Tough Questions

If you are stumped on a problem or it appears too hard or too difficult, don't waste time. Move on! Remember though, if you can quickly check for obviously incorrect answer choices, your chances of guessing correctly are greatly improved. Before you completely give up, at least try to knock out a couple of possible answers. Eliminate what you can and then guess at the remaining answer choices before moving on.

⊘ Check Your Work

Since you will probably not know every term listed and the answer to every question, it is important that you get credit for the ones that you do know. Don't miss any questions through careless mistakes. If at all possible, try to take a second to look back over your answer selection and make sure you've selected the correct answer choice and haven't made a costly careless mistake (such as marking an answer choice that you didn't mean to mark). This quick double check should more than pay for itself in caught mistakes for the time it costs.

⊘ Pace Yourself

It's easy to be overwhelmed when you're looking at a page full of questions; your mind is confused and full of random thoughts, and the clock is ticking down faster than you would like. Calm down and maintain the pace that you have set for yourself. Especially as you get down to the last few minutes of the test, don't let the small numbers on the clock make you panic. As long as you are on track by monitoring your pace, you are guaranteed to have time for each question.

⊘ Don't Rush

It is very easy to make errors when you are in a hurry. Maintaining a fast pace in answering questions is pointless if it makes you miss questions that you would have gotten right otherwise. Test writers like to include distracting information and wrong answers that seem right. Taking a little extra time to avoid careless mistakes can make all the difference in your test score. Find a pace that allows you to be confident in the answers that you select.

⊘ Keep Moving

Panicking will not help you pass the test, so do your best to stay calm and keep moving. Taking deep breaths and going through the answer elimination steps you practiced can help to break through a stress barrier and keep your pace.

Final Notes

The combination of a solid foundation of content knowledge and the confidence that comes from practicing your plan for applying that knowledge is the key to maximizing your performance on test day. As your foundation of content knowledge is built up and strengthened, you'll find that the strategies included in this chapter become more and more effective in helping you quickly sift through the distractions and traps of the test to isolate the correct answer.

Now that you're preparing to move forward into the test content chapters of this book, be sure to keep your goal in mind. As you read, think about how you will be able to apply this information on the test. If you've already seen sample questions for the test and you have an idea of the question format and style, try to come up with questions of your own that you can answer based on what you're reading. This will give you valuable practice applying your knowledge in the same ways you can expect to on test day.

Good luck and good studying!

Creating, Performing, and Producing Theater

Directing and Producing Theatrical Productions

Production Meeting

A production meeting is often held after the play is selected. It can occur before and/or after the actors are selected. The actors can be a part of the meeting or not depending on the director. This meeting allows the director to meet with the theatre staff and technicians to determine how the production will be laid out. The director relays his vision to the set designers, being careful to do so in a manner that will allow the designers the freedom to interpret and create the layout themselves. It is important for the director to provide a focus for the group while allowing each member to contribute in their unique way. The director can elaborate upon his vision and clarify what his exact needs are for the production. The group provides feedback on what they can or cannot do based on the director's expectations.

Heretical Approach to Directing

According to the heretical approach to directing, the director's job is to interpret the script to create a dramatic production that will be enjoyed by an audience. The director must work to make a script exciting to the audience. This approach requires that directors interpret the script, maintaining its overall meaning while exercising creative freedom to alter an ending or omit certain scenes. This approach can be seen in classical works that are translated to opera. English-born doctor Thomas Bowdler used this approach to rewrite the works of Shakespeare, omitting what he saw as offensive or unsuitable parts. He called his book The Family Shakespeare, as he believed he had transformed Shakespeare's work so that a father could read it to his children without fear of corrupting them. Directors may use this approach, though it is most often associated with a prudish censorship that does not lend itself to the theatre.

History of Directing

In ancient Greece the modern director's role was performed by a **choregus**. The choregus was the leader of the chorus and it was his job to direct and coordinate songs and movements. In ancient Roman theatre, productions were organized by a wealthy patron who provided the financing necessary for a performance. In medieval times, the role most closely related to that of the modern director was called the "master of secrets." The master of secrets was responsible for special effects and because of the detail and coordination required to perform these effects successfully and safely, he was essentially responsible for telling actors where to stand. In the period when actors had to register in order to perform, the director role was carried out by the keeper of the register. The register was an official copy of a script that was performed by a specific theatre company. The keeper of the register was usually a guild, or group of craftsmen, who were responsible for maintaining the integrity of the script by handing it down to each successive generation.

Modern Role of Director

Directors perform both artistic and managerial roles. The modern theatre director must interpret a script, cast actors, design the production, conduct rehearsals and coordinate a vast number of other tasks and elements. Oftentimes, interpreting a script requires the director's use of creative license. Directors must master human relations, as they work with actors, set designers and lighting crews to bring a script to life. Directors must be capable of making quick decisions while being able to adapt to change. Directors often act as business managers, publicity directors or even costume designers and they are skilled at working with the resources they have available to unify the various elements that comprise a dramatic production.

Coaching Actors

Due to the work of Konstantin Stanislavsky, it is now common for directors to collaborate with actors in order to create a successful performance. Directors can be encouraged to guide actors but should also be cautioned not to over-direct actors. This could lead to dependency, so it is usually best for the director to consult with the actor rather than instruct the actor. The director can be an advisor or a source of inspiration and encouragement for an actor. The actor and director each must recognize the other's creative talents and work together to incorporate their visions into a unified performance that leaves both parties, and the audience, feeling satisfied. The way in which the director cooperates with the actor can take many forms. Sometimes the director will assume one role and maintain it or perhaps fluctuate among different roles. Examples of these roles include the authoritarian, the visionary and the therapist.

Managerial Responsibilities

One of the many aspects of the director's role is that of manager. The director must serve both in an artistic capacity when interpreting a script and in a managerial capacity when organizing and coordinating the details of a performance. The director must handle scheduling, casting and rehearsals as well as conduct read-throughs in which the director and actors read the script and discuss their vision for the characters and design of the play. The director leads rehearsals, which can occur with all actors present to rehearse the entire play or with only a few actors rehearsing a portion of the play. The director leads run-throughs, technical rehearsals and dress rehearsals and may even conduct previews which involve executing a performance outside of the intended venue in order to discover any areas of the performance that need to be worked out before opening. The director's job usually ends after opening night, at which point the stage manager takes over.

Considerations When Selecting a Script for Study or Performance

When selecting a show for class use, whether it is to be read in class for instruction or evaluated for performance potential, teachers must consider several factors. First and foremost, it is imperative that teachers read the entirety of any script which they intend to bring before students. While pre-reading, they can evaluate whether or not the content meets community standards. A good way to evaluate this is to consider whether or not their administrator would be likely to approve a performance of this work. The teacher must also consider the age of their students, not only for whether certain themes are age-appropriate, but also whether the issues in the play would be valuable or important to the age group they are teaching. Related to this, teachers should seek out scripts that reflect the cultural atmosphere of their school and local community. While theatre can be an excellent tool for broadening horizons, it is also important to promote representation of the culture students are rooted in. A final consideration is how the student body would perceive and relate to the script if it was performed for them. Considering whether the students would be challenged, inspired, offended, educated, or entertained by the show is a good first step.

Researching a Script or Playwright Prior to Selection

Prior to selecting a show for class study or production, teachers should do their research to ensure the script is the right fit for their students and community. An important aspect of this that can easily be overlooked is the background of the playwright. Since teachers will need to present the background information to the students, and eventually teach students to research the author's background themselves, they need to be familiar with the author's life so that they can answer any questions the students have and guide the conversation where necessary. It is also important to consider the historical time period and political climate, both in which the script was written and in which the action of the script is set. Depending on the age of students and demographics of your school, period pieces which discuss or involve civil rights may need careful discussion and consideration. Another aspect that must be evaluated carefully is whether or not there is potential for issues with dialogue or casting. While permission from the author or publisher to modify dialogue by striking lines or cutting scenes can be requested, it is not always granted. Identifying any potential issues early and keeping in mind that they may not be resolved by simply striking problematic lines is key.

Coordinating Efficient Rehearsal Schedules

When scheduling rehearsals, teachers should consult any calendars they can access for school and community events, as well as athletic schedules. While conflicts are certain to occur, it is in the best interest of the students to be as flexible as possible. Teachers should consider creating a policy outlining a reasonable attendance expectation which the students can review prior to auditioning. If teachers choose to implement such a policy, a good practice is requiring students to fill out a conflict sheet on which they can list any upcoming vacations, community events, family functions, etc. that they will need to be out for during the course of the show. Anything on this sheet must be counted as an "excused" absence. Teachers may choose to set the rehearsal schedule prior to auditions, or they may choose to set it after casting to accommodate the schedules of the students that have been cast. All rehearsal schedules must comply with any state and district limits on student time.

Considerations When Scheduling Theatrical Performances

Teachers are frequently responsible for scheduling theatrical performances, whether that means choosing a date themselves or coordinating with a district event scheduler. In either case, the teacher needs to take multiple things into account, including the district calendar, athletic schedules, community events, and time of year. While there is no way to find a perfect date which has no conflicts, it's important to try to remember that behind each event on the calendar is a group of people trying to do just what you're doing. Collaboration and grace are key when scheduling, particularly when dealing with so many schedules and needs.

Determining the Budget for a Theatrical Performance

In many districts, teachers will be given a budget for the school year which will fund all activities for the theatre program. In some districts, there may be a separate budget for classroom supplies, but this varies and should be discussed early on. Most theatre programs will participate in some type of fundraising throughout the year to supplement the annual district budget. Regardless of what the budget is, the teacher must evaluate the year and plan in advance in order to properly allocate spending. Some contracts have show requirements, which must also be taken into account. For example, if a teacher is working in a district which has a $6,000 budget for the theatre program, and requires a minimum of two shows per school year, the teacher could reasonably consider dividing the budget in half to have $3,000 per show. Another option would be to do a smaller show and a larger show, and divide up the money accordingly.

Promoting Theatrical Performances

Promotion of performances is one of the most important, yet frequently unplanned and overlooked aspects of planning a show. A cast can have a wonderful show, but without selling tickets, no one will know. It is exceedingly important to get people in the door to see shows both for fundraising and for recruitment. Ticket sales are often one of the primary ways to raise funds for the program, so a low-performing event can affect the budget for the rest of the year. When students and their families attend shows that are excellent, it is more likely that they will want to become involved in the theatre program. There are so many things to plan and take care of when directing a show that promotion is often overlooked to the detriment of a program.

Managing Skills Employed When Directing a Production

Being a theatre teacher requires a lot of different skills, many of which are managerial in nature. It is important for teachers to be able to manage a budget, keep a rehearsal schedule, help students deal with interpersonal conflicts in the cast and crew, delegate tasks when appropriate, oversee teams of students responsible for various tasks, and ensure the safety of each and every student in their cast and crew. Many of the same skills necessary for good classroom management are necessary for directing a performance, including fair and consistent procedures and policies, clear communication with both students and parents, self-awareness and strong emotional regulation, and empathy.

Knowledge of Legal Issues

Teachers must be aware of the royalties and copyright information legalities. When a teacher purchases the rights to perform a show, they typically sign a contract with the publisher of the script which includes terms of use and royalty information. The legal ramifications of breaking this contract vary by publisher and show, and must be read very carefully. If a teacher breaches the terms of the contract, they risk disqualification in any contest the show is entered in, tarnishing the reputation of their school, financial ramifications, and quite possibly, their position as the theatre teacher.

Emotional Well-Being in Technical Theatre

Preparing a production is an intense and time-consuming process that can prevent cast and crew from "having a life" outside of theatre. As such, it is important that there be an effort to help protect the emotional and mental wellbeing. Social-emotional learning and self-care techniques should be addressed by theatre teachers. This will provide students with tools they need to be aware of any changes in their feelings and how to address them. Theatre provides a platform for teaching about emotions and what they look and feel like. This helps students understand their own emotions as well as build empathy and understanding for others. It is important to help students find and maintain a balance in their lives between their education, hobbies, and resting. Teachers should familiarize themselves with the resources that are available to students that will help maintain their well-being, such as school counseling services. All school staff members should be trained to recognize changes in student behaviors and refer them to the proper channels for assistance; theatre teachers are no exception. For intense roles, students may need assistance learning to **de-role**, the process of getting oneself out of character. This can be as simple as removing a costume or playing a game, but can be more intensive such as exercise, meditating, or talking it out with a trusted individual.

Potential for Student Development

Teachers should evaluate performance pieces with an eye towards how students might be able to grow and learn more about the craft of theatre. An ideal experience with the theatre program would teach students about themselves, the world, and those around them. However, the potential for students to learn about topics that are not age-appropriate is extremely high in the theatre world. Many directors succumb to the temptation to give their students material that is dramatic or interesting, but which contains themes that students might not be ready to be exposed to yet. Particularly in middle school, students are already facing extreme emotions, and teachers should take great caution before selecting any scripts which contain sensitive topics and themes.

Influences on the Selection of Works for Performance

Cultural Diversity of a Student Body

Teachers must consider the cultural diversity of their potential cast when seeking out a show. It is very important to present opportunities for all students who might be interested, and sometimes the concept of "color-blind casting" isn't enough to encourage students to audition. A teacher might clearly tell students that they will not be considering race as an audition element, but choose a script that feels limiting. For example, an African American student might not feel comfortable auditioning for a historically white role like Fanny Brice in Funny Girl. Even though a teacher has communicated they will be utilizing color-blind casting, if the script they select doesn't align with the cultural diversity of the student body, students might not feel that there is a place for them in the program. Students may feel more uncomfortable challenging a role's historical precedence with famous works, especially those that have movie adaptations.

Cultural Diversity Presented in the Script

When selecting a performance piece, teachers should consider whether or not their student body can accurately and appropriately depict the cultural diversity presented in the source material. For example, a program with an extremely small Hispanic or Latino population might not be the right fit for a show such as West Side Story. While a show such as this would likely be a great learning opportunity, the teacher would need to cautiously consider whether they would be able to respectfully depict the racial tension in the show without making their Hispanic or Latino students feel more marginalized. On the other hand, Hispanic students might enjoy the opportunity to play characters from their own heritage, so this show might be an excellent choice for a school with a group of Hispanic or Latino students that love performing. Shows that contain cultural diversity can be excellent choices, but teachers must consider all factors carefully, and seek guidance from administrators, before making final decisions.

Characteristics of a Potential Audience

When selecting a performance piece, teachers must consider the potential audience that will be watching the show. In a school setting, the most likely scenario is that the audience will be full of students' family members. This might be parents, grandparents, or younger siblings, so a range of ages needs to be taken into account. The general atmosphere of the community also needs to be considered. For example, if a school is in a more conservative community, shows with liberal elements should be approached cautiously (if at all). Fellow teachers and administrators, as well as school board members, might also be members of the potential audience. While these factors should not completely dictate the show selection, they should be considered.

The Performance Space and Number of Participants

Before selecting a show, teachers must consider the space they will be performing in as well as the number of participants they might have. Most teachers will be able to look around their performance space prior to choosing a show. They should take note of the size of the stage, the amount of backstage space, storage space, amount of dressing rooms and restrooms, and number of seats in the audience. Teachers should also have a general idea of how many students are interested in participating. The number of students auditioning should influence the size of the show the teacher plans. For example, if 20 students are interested in auditioning, the teacher should consider shows with casts of 10-12 people. (There will inevitably be students that change their minds, auditions that go poorly, and students that drop out unexpectedly.)

Casting

Audition Methods

Theatre teachers need to assess many different skills when holding auditions for a show or performance, including the following:

- Ability to memorize lines
- Vocal strength
- Physicality
- Portrayal of emotions

Some of the methods teachers may use to hold auditions are prepared monologues, cold readings, and improvisation. While all of these audition methods can be used successfully, they each present different opportunities for students to showcase their skills. Depending on the needs of the show, the time available, and the experience level of their students, teachers may choose to use only one of these methods in the auditions they hold, or they may mix and match.

Prepared Monologues

Asking students to perform a prepared monologue can be done in one of four ways. The teacher may:

- Preselect one monologue for all students to perform
- Provide a selection of monologues varying in length, tone, and genre for students to choose from
- Ask students to write their own monologue (particularly if this is a learning objective that has already been met in class)
- Allow students to choose their own monologue

Because prepared monologues are expected to be memorized before the audition date, students have the opportunity to display their ability to memorize and perform lines. Students are also able to take the time to do research about the scene the monologue is taken from, score the text appropriately, and practice how they will deliver the lines. A disadvantage of choosing monologues as an audition method is that, by nature, teachers only see a prepared performance, which means they cannot assess a student's theatrical instincts as much as their preparation methods. Another disadvantage is that students may get stuck in a mechanical performance mode, and feel unable to deviate from what they practiced even if they want to adjust once in the audition room.

Cold Readings

A **cold reading** occurs when teachers provide a text during an audition and ask students to perform it then and there. The text might be a dialogue or monologue from the show the student is auditioning from a different source. One advantage of this audition method is that students must rely heavily on their instincts and ability to quickly interpret the text. This allows teachers to assess how easily students derive meaning from the written lines. Parsing a characters' lines in order to determine their personality and backstory is something that almost all students must be taught. However, some students are naturally more adept at being able to pick up on aspects of a character when reading a scene, and this is a skill teachers will want to assess before casting them. A disadvantage of cold reading is that this method may present accessibility challenges for students with disabilities such as dyslexia or impaired vision, as it removes the opportunity to work with the text in a way that is comfortable and effective for them beforehand. This is particularly relevant for auditions that are open to the student body as a whole, as students that the teacher is unfamiliar with might show up. These students are not likely to self-disclose when handed a cold read, so the teacher may wrongly interpret their performance as displaying poor acting potential.

Review Video: Disorders that Impair Reading and Writing
Visit mometrix.com/academy and enter code: 306758

Improvisation

Improvisational theatre, also known as **improv**, occurs when the elements of a scene (setting, dialogue, characters, events) are unplanned. During an improv exercise, an actor spontaneously creates some or all of these elements with another actor. In an audition setting, a teacher may choose to give one or more of the elements of a scene to the student, or allow them free reign. Teachers may choose to align the improv exercise with some aspect of the play the student is auditioning for. An example of this would be asking the student to imagine that the character they are auditioning for is on a blind date, then play out that scene. Using improv as an audition method allows teachers to see how a student might respond to the unforeseen changes that inevitably happen during rehearsals and performances. One of the disadvantages of utilizing improv during an audition is that inexperienced actors frequently turn improvisational exercises into comedic scenes bordering on the ridiculous. Improv may also be overwhelming to beginning actors, and leave them feeling discouraged instead of empowered after an audition, regardless of how much advance prep work they put in.

Casting According to Learning Objectives

Before beginning the casting process, teachers should plan out which learning objectives they would like to cover while producing the show or performance. These may vary depending on which grade levels and types of theatre classes will be involved in the show. The objectives that are chosen should be communicated to the students in advance of the auditions. In many cases, an entire class will be involved in producing the show, but only some of the students will be in the cast and crew. For example, all of the students in theatre classes may help work on the set pieces, designing the costumes, and creating props during instructional class time even if only two of the students enrolled in that class are acting in the show. If planned well, this would allow the teacher to use the show as a vehicle for covering learning objectives regarding production, costuming, sets, and properties while encouraging a sense of ownership and excitement for each student in class. Teachers should also be aware that many states encourage nontraditional casting. Prior to casting, they should work towards a clear understanding of the standard for their individual schools in regards for casting non-traditionally.

Acting Methods and Performance

Elements of Acting

Relaxation, concentration, imagination, and observation:

There are several schools of thought about the qualities that one must either naturally possess or work to acquire in order to be an actor. The elements of relaxation, concentration, imagination and observation are most common among these qualities. An actor must maintain control of voice and body while performing and this ability is compromised by nervousness. Actors must learn to force their minds and bodies into a state of relaxation. Concentration allows the actor to focus attention on the desired outcome. Actors must use their voices and bodies in a way that conveys the essence of the character. An actor who is properly concentrating on the role will think about what they are doing rather than how they are doing it. Actors must also be mindful of the full range of human emotion. They must observe the manifestations of emotions in themselves and others and use these memories while performing. The actor should also be able to imagine the joys and sufferings of their characters, conveying that through performance.

Preparing for Performance

Psychologically and Emotionally

The concept of the "magic if" is often an effective tool used by actors. The magic if theory requires that actors imagine they are in the character's situation. These scenarios can be played out in two ways. Actors can be themselves but act as if they were in the same situation as characters or they can act as if they are the characters. In the first method, actors react to the situation personally. Once they have mastered their own personal reactions, actors can then analyze their reactions and examine how these compare to what the character would do in that situation. By combining the two reactions actors can often give the most believable performance. It is also helpful to draw upon sense memory and emotional memory to be able to depict a realistic emotion or reaction during a performance.

Alexander Technique

The Alexander Technique was developed by Shakespearean orator and actor Frederick Matthias Alexander. The technique arose from Alexander's desire to overcome his chronic laryngitis. Alexander discovered that he held unnecessary muscular tension while performing which caused his vocal problems. His technique requires that actors become aware of the tension they hold in their necks while performing. By releasing the neck tension, the head relaxes and allows the spine to remain long and uncompressed. This simple physical alignment results in an overall healthy condition of the body. The technique attempts to rid the body of tension and stress through the alteration of one's daily physical movements. Tension blocks an actor's ability to effectively portray the characters and stories in a performance. Studying the **Alexander Technique** can help an actor to reduce the amount of tension in their bodies and better understand how energy should be allocated to certain tasks in order to most efficiently accomplish one's goals in both acting and daily life.

James-Lange Theory of Emotion

The **James-Lange theory** was developed by psychologist William James and physiologist Carl Lange. The theory states that emotions are a result of physiological response to external stimuli. Our emotions, according to this theory, are based on our interpretations of physical sensation. For example, if we are at the beach and see a shark while swimming, our body becomes tense and our heart races. We interpret these physical reactions as fear. The theory suggests that emotion is not the cause of a physical response, but the result. This can be incorporated into acting techniques by having students describe or act out physical symptoms while other students guess the corresponding emotion. Nervous actors may also be taught to physically force themselves to relax, which, according to this theory, would result in a more calm emotional state. The theory can also be used to predict emotional reactions after observing one's physical behavior.

Cannon-Bard Theory of Emotion

The **Cannon-Bard theory** was developed by psychologists Walter Cannon and Philip Bard. Their theory states that emotion results in a physiological response, suggesting that our emotional reaction to external stimuli in turn leads to a physiological reaction. For example, feeling fearful may cause our heart to race and our body to tremble. This theory is in direct opposition of the James-Lange theory, which suggests that emotion is the result of physiological reaction and not the cause. The Cannon-Bard theory states that one must feel an emotion before the body can physiologically react. This theory can be incorporated into acting techniques by having students participate in scenarios that may make them fearful, anxious, angry or excited and then having them describe the physiological symptoms which accompanied each emotion.

Delsarte System of Expression

Francois Delsarte is best known for his system of expression involving the holding of specific poses to convey emotion or attitudes. The method was used in the first acting school founded in the United States. Delsarte began his career as a disgruntled student at the Paris Conservatory. Unsatisfied with the conservatory's acting classes, Delsarte began to independently study human movement and behavior. He also studied anatomical medicine, voice, breath and body language. All of his observations were conducted with the aim of understanding the role played by these various components as tools of instinctual and emotional expression. Delsarte's work was introduced to the US by his protégé, Steele Mackaye. Delsarte's system consists of nine principles of gesture, the relationship of inner experience and physical manifestation and the symbolism of various lines and their connection to human awareness.

Meisner Technique

The goal of the Meisner technique has often been described as getting actors to "live truthfully under imaginary circumstances." The technique emphasizes carrying out an action truthfully on stage and letting emotion and subtext build based on the truth of the action and on the other characters around them, rather than simply playing an action or emotion. One of the most well known exercises of the **Meisner Technique** is called **Repetition**. In Repetition, one person spontaneously makes a comment based on their partner's behavior, and that phrase would be repeated back and forth between the two in the same manner until it changed on its own. The objective is always to react truthfully and not merely change because it felt like change was called for.

Acting Terms

- **Articulation**: the ability to clearly pronounce words while acting or performing.
- **Blocking**: the development of the movements of actors on stage in relation to other actors and scenery/props.
- **Catharsis**: the purging of an emotion, such as fear or grief, which can occur while performing on stage.
- **Concentration**: the ability of an actor to be "in character" through use of dialogue, attitude, voice, costume, expressions and mannerisms.
- **Cold reading**: reading a script for the first time.
- **Context**: the conditions or climate in which a play was written or meant to be performed.
- **Cue**: signal that serves as an indicator of another action that is about to occur.
- **Denouement** occurs when the final conflict in a production is resolved.
- **Diction** is the choice of words that actors use to express themselves.
- **Downstage** is the physical location on the stage that is closest to the audience.
- **Emotional memory** is a tool used by actors in which they use their own specific memories of events in which they reacted emotionally to understand the emotions of the character they are portraying.
- A **dramaturg** is a specialist in theatre who may be called upon to advise actors, directors and producers in certain aspects of theatrical productions.
- **Exposition** occurs when one must provide information regarding the facts of the plot, usually to the audience either before or during a performance.
- **Level** is the height of an actor's head in a performance while carrying out certain actions.

Role-Playing

In **role-playing**, participants adopt and act out the roles of characters, or parts, that may have personalities, motivations, and backgrounds different from their own. Role-playing is like being in an improvisational drama or free-form theater in which the participants are the actors and the audience. People use the phrase "role-playing" in at least three distinct ways:

1. To refer to the playing of roles generally such as in a theater, or educational setting.
2. To refer to a wide range of games including computer role-playing games, play-by-mail games and more.
3. To refer specifically to role-playing games.

Children's Games

Children's games that involve role-play generally require no specific props and have no rules other than to stay in character. They are normally fun and can sometimes also serve the purpose of allowing children to explore adult roles and relationships. Play can reveal a lot about a child's psychological state, perception of gender roles, home life and interpretation of the world around them. Examples of common games include:

- *Cowboys & Indians*: This game remains popular around the world, even though the films, television series, and books that might have been thought to give rise to it have largely fallen from prominence. This gives an insight into the child's perception of good and evil.
- *Cops & Robbers*: Similar to Cowboys & Indians, seen by some as the politically correct version.
- *House*: The main aim is to explore familial relationships. Children can act like a family and explore other family arrangements with each other. It also deals with gender roles.
- *Shopkeeper and Customer*: This is interpretation of basic social interaction and can also be an insight into the child's parent's income status.

Improvisational Theatre Tradition

Another role-playing tradition is the improvisational theatre tradition. This goes back in some sense to the Commedia dell'Arte tradition of 16th century. Modern improvisational theatre began in the classroom with the "theatre games" of Viola Spolin and Keith Johnstone in the 1950s. Viola Spolin, who was one of the founders the famous comedy troupe Second City, insisted that her exercises were games, and that they involved role-playing, as early as 1946. She thought of these exercises as training actors and comics rather than as being primarily aimed at being fun in their own right.

Historical Re-Enactment

Role-playing in the form of historical re-enactment has been practiced by adults for millennia as well. The ancient Romans, the Han Chinese and medieval Europeans all enjoyed occasionally organizing events in which everyone pretended to be from an earlier age, and entertainment appears to have been the primary purpose of these activities. Within the 20th century, historical reenactment was often pursued as a hobby.

Puppets

A **puppet** is a representational object manipulated by a puppeteer. It is usually but not always a depiction of a human character and is used in a play or a presentation. The puppet undergoes a process of transformation through being animated and is normally manipulated by one (or sometimes more than one) puppeteer. Some puppets can be moved electronically. Puppets are made of a wide range of materials, depending upon the effect required and the amount of usage intended, and can be extremely complex or very simple in their construction. In contemporary visual or puppet theatre, puppets are often called "performing objects." There are many different varieties of puppets. Puppeteer Anita Sinclair states, "Through puppetry we accept the outrageous, the absurd or even the impossible, and will permit puppets to say and do things no human could. We allow a puppet to talk to us when no one else can get us to speak. We allow a puppet to smile at us even when we have not been introduced. We also allow a puppet to touch us when a person would lose an arm for the same offence." Puppeteer David Logan states, "Puppetry is a highly effective and dynamically creative means of exploring the richness of interpersonal communication. By its very nature, puppetry concentrates on the puppet rather than the puppeteer. This provides a safety zone for the puppeteer and allows for exploration of unlimited themes through a safe and non-threatening environment for communication."

MASKED PERFORMANCE

Throughout the world masks are used for their expressive power as a feature of masked performance. They are a familiar and vivid element in many folk and traditional pageants, ceremonies, rituals and festivals, many of which are of an ancient origin. The mask is often a part of costume that adorns the whole body and represents a tradition important to a particular society of people. Used almost universally, masks maintain their power and mystery both for their wearers and their audience, retaining an important place in the religious and social life of the community. The continued popularity of wearing masks at carnivals, and for children at parties and for festivals such as Halloween are reminders of the enduring power of pretense and play. The mask is also used in theatrical performance. In many cultural traditions, the masked performer is a central concept and is highly valued. In the western tradition it is sometimes considered a stylistic device, which can be traced back to the Greeks and Romans. Ancestors of the modern clown can be traced to the masked characters of the Commedia dell'Arte. In contemporary western theatre the mask is often used alongside puppetry to create a theatre that is essentially visual rather than verbal. Many of its practitioners have been visual artists.

MASKS

A **mask** is an artefact normally worn on the face, typically for protection, concealment, performance or amusement. Masks have been used since antiquity for both ceremonial and practical purposes. They are usually, but not always, worn on the face, although they may also be positioned for effect elsewhere in relation to the wearer's own head.

The word mask came via French masque and either Italian maschera or Spanish máscara. The 5000-year-old Sumerian mask of Warka, believed to be the oldest surviving mask, was looted from the Iraqi National Museum in Baghdad and recovered in 2003.

CLOWNS

Clowns are comic performers, stereotypically characterized by their colored wigs, stylistic makeup, outlandish costumes and unusually large footwear. Clowning, in its most basic form, can be described as one form of drama without a fourth wall. In other words, a clown acknowledges his audience. The clown's humor today is often visual and includes many elements of physical comedy or slapstick humor.

HISTORY OF CLOWNING

Clowning is a form of entertainment that has appeared in some manner in virtually every culture. In most cultures the clown is a ritual character associated with festivals or rites of passage and is often very different from the most popular western form. In Europe, up until as late as the 19th century the clown was a typical everyday character and often appeared in carnivals. The performance is symbolic of liminality. Being outside the rules of regular society, the clown is able to subvert the normal order. This basic premise is contemporarily used by many activists to point out social absurdity. A popular early form of clown was the fool, a role that can be traced back as far as ancient Egypt and appears as the first card in the Tarot deck. Most fools suffered from some physical or mental deformity, and were given to the local landlord as a charge because their families were unable to look after them. The surrounding communities often feared them. They were the butt of jokes and their masters had the power to inflict violence upon them, even taking their lives. However, being perceived 'idiots,' they were often the only people in court who enjoyed free speech, and during the 16th century, especially in France, actors began to train as fools often in order to have the ability to make satirical comment. There is evidence of the 'wise fool,' similar in function to the jester, in many other cultures.

Clowns of this era and eras previous to it were also associated with jugglers, who were seen as pariahs of society alongside actors, prostitutes and lepers, and thus (at least in Europe) wore stripes, or motley - cloth associated with marginalized people such as the condemned, with strong associations with the devil. Jugglers often used clowning techniques, and the later court jesters often danced, performed acrobatics and juggled. During the 16th century the Commedia dell'arte also became a huge influence on perceptions of the clown in Europe, and influence which passed through pantomime, into vaudeville and on to the touring circuses of the 19th and 20th centuries. The Commedia took influences from the grotesque masked clowns of carnivals and mystery plays and began in market places as a way to sell vegetables. It became incredibly popular throughout Europe amongst both the general public and the courts. The stock characters of the commedia originally included the Zanni - peasant clowns, Pantalone, the old Miser, Il Dottore - The Banal Doctor, and then grew from there to incorporate the Lovers, Arlecchino, Pedrolino, and Brighella, who have survived into the twentieth century in one form or another.

Mime

A **mime** is an actor who communicates entirely by gesture and facial expression. He mimics or imitates (a person or manner), especially for satirical effect. ("The actor mimicked the President very accurately.") He may also act out with gestures and bodily movements only, using no words. ("The acting students mimed eating an apple.") A mime gives a performance using gestures and body movements without words.

Terms Related to Show Preparation, Actors, and Performances

- The **acting edition** refers to the script that contains notes for actors or technicians and may be written by the playwright or the premiere production staff.
- **Ad lib** occurs when an actor must improvise lines or actions to compensate for forgetting their own or for another actor's lapse in memory.
- **Aria**: solo performance in an opera that conveys the emotional state of the main character.
- An **aside** occurs when an actor speaks directly to the audience, though the other characters are not privy to the information being shared.
- **Avista**: scene changes that are done in view of the audience.
- **Bastard prompt**: used in situations where the prompt corner must be stage right instead of stage left.
- **Beginners** term shouted by stage management to signify it is time for the actors who appear in the first scene to come onto the stage.
- **Bit part**: a very small role in a performance.
- **Book**: may refer to a prompt book or to the unsung parts of a musical.
- **Bump**: sudden flash of light often used as a cue.

- **Call**: a request that an actor come to stage to prepare for entrance into a scene.
- **Calling the show**: giving verbal cues to lighting-, sound- and fly- operators, as well as stage crew throughout a performance.
- **Catharsis**: occurs at the emotional climax of the play when the characters and the audience can achieve emotional cleansing.
- **Cheat**: an actor's movement without the audience's knowledge.
- **Clearance**: message to stage management from house manager to let them know that the house is ready for the performance to begin.
- **Come down**: refers to the closing time of a show.
- **Crossover**: the path an actor takes from one side of the stage to the other.
- **Curtain speech**: refers to a speech given by a director or theatre owner before a performance begins.
- **Denouement**: the moments in a performance when the point of the plot is revealed or explained.
- **Dialect coach**: specialist brought in to assist actors with specific accents necessary for conversations within the production.
- **Exposition**: background information on the characters or the plot of the play, usually occurring at the beginning of the play.
- **Fourth wall**: the imaginary wall that separates the audience and actors.
- **Half**: a term that stage management shouts to actors backstage when the show will begin in thirty minutes.
- **Interval**: a 15-20 minute break between sections of a performance.
- **Intonation**: the emphasis of certain words during any oral recitation.
- **On the book**: term used to refer to an actor who must use a script during a scene.
- **Places**: a term called out by directors when it is time for actors to stand in their appropriate positions to begin a scene.
- **Preproduction**: refers to the time before a production in which the planning is done.
- **Preview**: performances that occur prior to opening night.
- **Principals**: refers to the main actors in a production.
- **Prompter**: theatre's staff member who follows the script as the play is performed, standing ready to remind an actor of a line in the event they forget during a performance.
- **Quarter**: a term that stage management shouts to actors backstage when the show will start in fifteen minutes.
- **Quick change**: costume change that must happen so quickly that it must be done near the side of the stage instead of completely backstage.
- **Repertoire**: theatrical company organization in which two or more productions are alternated throughout the performing season.
- **Reprise**: term used in musicals to refer to the repetition of a song or dance at a later point in the show.
- **Run**: refers to the number of times a production is scheduled to show.
- **Segue**: used in musicals to refer to the act or scene that immediately follows another.
- **Show report**: report provided by stage management detailing any problems from the previous performance; actors and technical staff receive copies so that problems can be addressed.
- **Snap**: refers to a cue that has no fade time; usually a lighting or sound cue.
- **Soliloquy**: refers to an oration by an actor on stage when they are speaking to themselves.
- **Stagger-through**: the first run-through of a performance.

- **TBC**: acronym that stands for to be confirmed; usually seen in a cast list when an actor has not been chosen for a part or if a venue or date has not yet been selected.
- **Transformation**: refers to an immediate scene change that involves the use of gauze and lighting to hide or show certain areas of the stage.
- **Typecast**: term used to refer to an actor who is repeatedly cast in a similar role.
- **Visual cue**: a cue based on the action on stage rather than given by a stage manager.
- **Walk-on**: acting role that requires the actor be physically present on stage but not speak.

Scripting

Analyzing and Interpreting a Script

A director must analyze a script in order to gain an understanding of the text's overall structure and theme. The director must carefully study the function of each character in the script. Once they understand the hierarchy of the characters, they must consider how that will translate into demands for the actor. The director must consider the script's technical requirements, including lighting, costumes and sound. The director must take into consideration the time period in which the play was written compared to the time period in which the script takes place. Directors must be able to read the script and gather information regarding the context and subtext of the work. It may also be helpful for a director to understand the biography of the playwright as well as be familiar with some of their other works.

Tone and Impact

When reviewing a script, a director must identify several elements to determine, given his resources, whether the script is suitable for performance. Directors look for certain details in the script that lend to the overall tone of a performance and they must identify the elements in the script that will bring the play to life. Ranking the importance of each element and determining if the overall tone of the play would be strengthened or weakened by manipulating those elements is also important. These elements include light, sound, setting, props, language and costumes. It is easy to manipulate these elements, since character, idea, and story are integral to the story and should generally remain unchanged. The director should identify the peaks of excitement in a script and build upon these to bring energy and dynamic structure to the play.

Script Analysis

Beckerman believed that a play script was like a musical score. Musical scores indicate the sounds that are played by a human or instrument, whereas a script indicates the shape of the energy that is to be expressed by a person. Beckerman identified and termed many elements of a script. He referred to the person exerting energy as the "impelling agent." The impelling agent exerts energy in an effort to achieve a goal, which Beckerman terms the "project." The impelling agent encounters many obstacles in pursuit of the project and Beckerman terms these obstacles "resistance." Beckerman also believed that a play should be broken into units which he called segments. Each segment consists of an impelling agent overcoming resistance to complete a project.

The Dynamics of Drama

Beckerman's method of script analysis, when first introduced, was different from all other approaches. The standard script analysis required one to identify the elements of a script including character, plot, setting and theme. This method forced the interpreter to view the play from the outside as though all of its parts existed simultaneously, but this is not the manner in which a play is performed or viewed. Beckerman reasoned that this should not be the way a script is analyzed. Rather, his method of analysis requires that the script be broken into units called "segments." In each segment the impelling agent completes a project. The project may be as simple as exerting energy that helps actors/characters psychologically adjust to the changes around them.

Active and Reactive Segments

In Bernard Beckerman's book The Dynamics of Drama he states that script analysis should involve breaking a script into segments. Each segment consists of an impelling agent exerting force to overcome resistance, resulting in the completion of a project. A segment can be termed "active" if the agent is exerting force externally. Active segments are goal-oriented and require the agent to perform an action to complete the project. A "reactive" segment is produced when an agent must exert energy internally in order to emotionally or psychologically adjust to a change. Reactive segments generally consist of an agent who experiences a change rather than creates one.

Crux and Decrescence

Beckerman's treatment of script analysis requires that the script be broken into segments. Each segment consists of an impelling agent exerting energy to overcome resistance resulting in the completion of a project. Segments may be active or reactive depending on the type of energy the agent is required to exert. In each segment there is a point at which it becomes clear whether the resistance or the project will be the prevailing force. This point is called the **crux**. The crux is the point at which a dramatic shift of power occurs between the resistance and the project. Each segment ends in what is called the **decrescence**. The decrescence is the change or reaction to the change that has been brought about by the crux. The decrescence is the agent's response to the prevalence of either the resistance or project.

Costumes and Makeup

Costume Designing

The costume designer's role is very important in helping to achieve the director's vision. The costumes should contribute to the tone and style of a production and the time period in which the play is set must be taken into account. It is important to consider the many facets of a character's personality and lifestyle, including their job and social status. The costumes also serve to differentiate or unify certain characters. For example, a play in which the characters are divided between servants and the aristocracy should involve two distinct costuming groups. Costumes must also be practical for the actors, allowing them to move freely and change quickly. It is important for costume designers to consult with the director in order to ensure that the costume designs will be consistent with the theme of the production.

Functions of Costumes in Theatrical Productions

Costumes serve many functions in a production, including the formation of a character, clarity of time and place, and the creation of an immersive environment. Costume pieces come together to create a visual for the actors and the audience. Many actors say they can't fully be in character until their costume is on. Part of the rationale for this is that the costumes help create the setting of the show, and may make the transition into a role smoother. Costuming provides clarity for the time and place of the show, because the visuals are already there rather than having to be imagined. For example, if a show is set in 1920, one could imagine a setting fairly well due to pop culture depictions. However, a show set in 1750 might be a bit more challenging to accurately imagine. Costuming can help take the guesswork out and provide concrete details for the audience and actors.

Construction Techniques for Creating Costumes

Prior to beginning costume construction, it is critical to fully understand the costume needs of the project. This will first begin by understanding the setting of the production. Period pieces will likely require more effort in costume sourcing than productions set in the current time-period. The costume designer should then thoroughly read the script and take note of costume needs. For example, if a scene requires an actor to remove an article of clothing, such as a coat or gloves, the designer will need to ensure these pieces are part of the costume design. Following the script read, measurements need to be taken of the actors to ensure costume pieces will fit. With all the aforementioned information, the designer can begin plotting costumes. This includes sketching costumes, creating vision boards, and obtaining sample pieces. Once a final vision has been established, the designer will begin to make, buy, or rent costume pieces. These decisions are typically made based on cost and availability. For modern productions, it is usually easiest to purchase most pieces while productions set in different eras will likely require more pieces be made. For elaborate or expensive articles of clothing, renting is a more cost and time effective option than buying or making.

Obtaining Costumes

Costumes are obtained in four main ways: buying new costume pieces, renting from a store or neighboring company, constructing pieces, or thrifting pieces. Buying new costume pieces is often the easiest, but most expensive, method. Teachers who choose this route can get appropriate measurements from their cast members and purchase clothes that exactly fit these measurements. Sometimes stores carry rentable costumes, and while this may be cheaper than buying new, it may be harder to find exactly what teachers are looking for.

1. On occasion, a neighboring school or company might have a costume shop they are willing to rent from, but this is far from a sure solution.
2. Constructing costume pieces is a creative solution, but one that takes a lot of time and energy. For this option to work, teachers must have seamstress and perhaps even millinery experience, or they must be willing to learn.
3. Teachers that have a section of Technical Theatre students may be able to teach their students some basic sewing skills to help shoulder the burden, but this is also not a perfect solution.
4. The final strategy for sourcing costumes is thrifting. This can be accomplished by going to local garage sales, secondhand clothing shops, thrift stores, or even using social media to post what a teacher is in need of to see if any friends or colleagues have something similar in their closets.

Most programs use some combination of the four of these techniques.

Types of Stage Makeup

There are many types of stage makeup, but they can be broken down into the following groups: alcohol-based, cream-based, powder-based, wax-based, and water-based. The cost and ease of use vary by type. Alcohol-based makeup must be activated with 99% alcohol, and is formulated to be long-lasting. Cream-based makeup, also known as "grease-paint," is typically oil-based and is very long lasting. This type of makeup is frequently packaged in stick form, and must be set with powder in order to stay on under hot lights. Powder-based makeup, also known as "cake" or "pancake" makeup, can be applied wet or dry, and is typically full-coverage. Wax-based makeup is buildable, and hypoallergenic. Water-based makeup must be activated with water, and is applied to the skin much like watercolor paint.

Suggesting Character and Communicating the Concept of the Production

Stage makeup is intended to combat the effects of the harsh stage lighting and distance from the stage for audience members, but must also be tailored to each individual actor or actress. When applying **stage makeup**, teachers must keep in mind what characteristics should be accentuated based on the role the student is playing. For example, if a character is a female villain, the teacher might choose to apply darker eyeshadow, a darker shade of lipstick, and more accentuated cheekbones. For a male villain, darker eyeliner, shadowy contouring, and a dark brown lip would be appropriate.

Techniques Used in Costume Construction

Constructing a costume will require a variety of skills that vary in difficulty, the most common being sewing. Sewing may be completed by hand or machine. There are several different types of stitches used in sewing to meet different needs. The most common is the **running stitch** in which two pieces of fabric are joined by the thread passing between them. When constructing a garment from scratch, the designer will select a fabric that meets their needs based on stretch and texture, the drape of the fabric, durability, and care requirements. The designer will also have to consider fastener needs. **Fasteners** include items like buttons, hooks and eyes, snaps, buckles, magnets, and pins that join parts of clothing. The type of fastener used will be determined by the way that pieces will be used. If it is an article that requires quick removal, the designer should go with an easy-to-use fastener like magnets or snaps over buttons or hooks and eyes. **Care** for costumes after they are worn and between uses will vary based on the delicacy of the item and fabric as well as the soil level of the individual articles. Delicate or heavily soiled pieces may need professional cleaning while other items can be washed in a standard washing machine.

Purpose of Cutting and Dying Fabric

Designing costumes from scratch requires a designer to select fabrics that meet their needs. In almost all cases, the fabric will need to be cut and in many it will require dying. When using existing articles of clothing, it may be necessary to alter the clothing to fit an actor or dye it to fit the needs of the production. A costume designer will use **fabric shears**, sharp scissors intended for cutting fabrics, as well as a **fabric cutter**, a rotary blade on a handle, for cutting fabric. When using those tools to cut pieces with a pattern, a designer may also use **textile weights** which help ensure there is no movement of the fabric or pattern. When dying fabrics, there are two general choices for the type of dye used: natural or synthetic. As the names suggest, **natural dyes** are made from natural resources like plants and minerals while **synthetic dyes** are made of chemicals. Both dyes work by saturating the fabric and creating a bond between the molecules in the dye and the fibers in the fabric.

Principles of Makeup Application When Utilizing Simple Prosthetics

The use of simple **prosthetics** such as bald caps, false noses, and ear tips is common in stage productions. Prior to applying prosthetics teachers should check the dates on all of their products to ensure they are still usable. Teachers should ensure that none of their students are allergic to latex. If a latex allergy is present, the severity of the allergy should be confirmed with parents. Latex alternatives include white glue, makeup wax, and silicon rubber. Silicon rubber is very difficult to work with, so the teacher should practice before attempting with a student. Teachers should ensure that they have plenty of gloves, spirit gum, non-latex sponges, makeup in the skin tones of all students, cotton balls, applicators, and makeup wipes. Students must be taught about appropriate removal methods so they don't over-exfoliate their skin. After use, reusable prosthetic pieces should be washed in warm soapy water, carefully dried, and stored away from extreme temperatures.

Safe Use and Care of Costumes and Makeup

All costumes should be properly laundered after each show, and should comfortably fit the student. If a costume becomes ill-fitting for any reason, it should be altered or replaced. It's important to check hem length, as well as how shoes are fitting. Depending on the age of the student, their shoe size may change fairly rapidly. Any student, cast member, or adult applying makeup needs to be trained in infection control procedures. Appropriate application materials (single use sponges, wands, foam applicators, etc.) must be provided and sanitized (makeup brushes for powders, implements such as tweezers, etc.) when necessary. All makeup should be selected by the teacher, as some makeup materials contain dangerous chemicals and additives. Students should not share makeup with one another, or use their personal makeup from home.

Creating Theatrical Environment with Costume Selection and Makeup

Costumes and makeup work together to create theatrical environments, particularly by influencing perception. The way a person dresses in real life causes them to be perceived in a certain way, and the same is true on the stage. Since audience members and fellow actors are interacting with the show in a visual way, the way things look influences the way they feel. For example, a character dressed simply with a clean appearance is likely to be more trustworthy than a character dressed in dirty or unkempt clothing with a grungy appearance. Each individual's costume and makeup comes together to form a general impression of the show, including setting, that creates an immersive environment.

Stages and Set Design

Stages

Most simply, a stage is the space where a dramatic production takes place. There are currently three major types of stages in use:

1. Theatre in the round or the arena stage allows the audience to surround the stage, which provides a much different dramatic experience for both players and audiences alike. Originally, this form of stage was used in classical theatre in Greece and Rome, and is widely used today in smaller experimental theaters around the world.
2. The apron or thrust stage seats audiences on the sides of a platform. Less commonly used today, Shakespeare's Globe Theatre was an early form of the apron stage.
3. The most common stage in current use is the proscenium stage where the audience sits in front of a stage framed by the acting space. This form is very common in drama, opera, and musical presentations.

The type of stage used affects the action of the dramatic work, and each offers a unique experience to the audience.

Stage Areas:

↔BACKSTAGE AREA↔

Stage Right	Up Stage Center	Stage Left
Center Stage Right	Center Stage	Center Stage Left
Down Stage Right	Down Stage Center	Down Stage Left

↔AUDIENCE SEATING↔

Set Design

Tools for Modeling

Modern set designers are able to utilize a variety of modeling software to create set designs and layouts, but design software can be costly and difficult to learn. More primitive methods that are still very common include renderings. A rendering is a free-hand drawing of a set based on the first impressions of the designer or director. The renderings rarely ever represent a complete idea and are changed throughout preproduction. Designers may also create a set using a ground plan, which is a drawing of the set design from above the stage looking directly down. This allows the designer to gauge the space between items on the stage. Set designers may also use three-dimensional models and thumbnail sketches. Scale drawings of the set are called elevations and are commonly used in set design.

Mise-en-Scene

Mise-en-scene is a French term that translates as "put in the scene." The term refers to everything that is placed upon a stage to be filmed or shown as part of a performance. The term can refer to actors, scenery, lighting and costumes. It can refer to the manner in which the performance space is utilized or to the movements of the actors in relation to the scenery. It is a very all-encompassing term. Scholars agree that the term can take on various meanings and some feel that mise-en-scene is better defined as the emotional tone of a film.

Terms Relating to the Theater, Stage, and Audience

- The **acting area** is the space on a stage or in another performance space in which an actor can move while remaining in full view of the audience.
- **Apron**: the section of a stage that projects into the auditorium.
- **Black box**: a studio theatre, usually surrounded by black curtains, in which the audience and actors share space.
- **Curtain line**: either the imaginary line across the stage where the curtain would be if it were closed or to the final spoken line in a play.
- **Dark**: term used when referring to a venue that has been closed either permanently or temporarily between productions.
- **FOH**: front of house.

- **Forestage**: part of a stage that projects outward into the auditorium.
- **Found space**: a theatre space suitable for performances but not originally designed to be a theatre.
- **House**: can refer to the theatre auditorium or to the audience in the theatre.
- **House manager**: member of the theatre staff who is responsible for ensuring the health and safety of audience members during a performance.
- **In the round**: a theatre layout in which the acting stage is entirely encircled by audience seating.
- **Opening the house**: when stage management alerts the FOH staff that the stage is set and the audience can begin taking their seats.
- **Papering the house**: a marketing technique in which tickets are given away to make a show seem to be selling better than it actually is.
- **Pass door**: door that is located in the wall of the proscenium arch, which acts as a passage between the auditorium and stage.
- **Passarelle**: walkway that allows actors to get close to audience via a path beyond the proscenium arch into the orchestra pit.
- **Pit**: refers to the area of a theatre in which the orchestra is seated.
- **Pit net**: net placed over the pit area of the theatre to prevent actors and objects from falling into the area where the orchestra is be located.
- **Platform stage**: usually refers to an acting stage that is lifted from the floor in a space that was not created as a theatre.
- **Promenade**: a theatrical arrangement in which the audience moves around the acting area to see the performance from multiple locations.
- **Prompt**: side-generally refers to the left side of the stage or whichever side the prompt corner is located.
- **Proscenium arch**: refers to the frame through which the audience sees a performance; usually the wall opening between the stage and auditorium.
- **Raked auditorium**: refers to audience seating that is arranged in a forward sloping manner.
- **Raked stage**: refers to a stage that slopes upwards towards the upstage or back end.
- **Receiving house**: venue that hosts incoming touring companies.
- **Scene shop**: section of the theatre where technicians and designers construct scenery.
- **Sightlines**: lines that are drawn on plans and diagrams to identify the areas of the stage that are visible to the extreme seating areas of the audience.
- **Stage door keeper**: a member of the theatrical crew, positioned inside the stage door whose role is to know each actor and member of the technical staff, know fire safety procedures for the theatre, greet visitors and press, and pass messages between any parties.
- **Stalls**: refers to the audience's seating that is just below stage level.
- **Thrust**: refers to a stage that reaches forward into the auditorium and has audience seating on at least two sides; also called a theatre in the round.
- **Tormentors**: screens or curtains that are usually set up at right angles to the proscenium arch to keep the audience from seeing activity occurring off-stage.
- **Traverse**: theatre set-up in which the audience is seated on either side of the acting area.
- **Trap**: an opening built into the stage floor.
- **Grave trap**: a rectangular drop-down, resembling a grave, built into a stage floor.
- **Cauldron trap**: a trap built into a stage floor to facilitate placing items into a prop (such as a cauldron) from beneath the stage.

- **Star trap**: refers to a trap that has multiple triangular hinged doors through which an actor can enter the stage from below.
- **Trap room**: the room directly under the trap door of a stage.
- **Treads**: refers to stairs or steps connected to a stage area.
- **Upper circle**: usually raked seating in a theatre, located at the highest level in the auditorium.
- **Upstage**: refers to the part of the acting stage that is farthest away from the audience seating; may also be used to refer to the undesirable movement of one actor while on stage that causes another actor to turn their back towards the audience.
- **Ushers**: theatre staff members who lead audience to their seats; ushers are often seated in the auditorium during performances in case of an emergency.
- **Vomitory**: entrance to the auditorium located in the banked seating areas.
- **Wings**: the sides of the stage that are not in the audience's line of sight; may also refer to scenery that is set up at the point where the acting area meets the technical area.

Staging a Play

Staging a play is the process of determining where actors should physically be located at various points in the play. The aim of this exercise is to ensure that the position of the actors achieves the desired visual focus. The actors, props, set and lighting need to all work together to focus the audience's attention to the right place at the right time. Staging a play also involves blocking, which is pinpointing where the actors should be situated on stage. Staging a play also involves coordinating stage business, which is any activity that takes place on stage during a performance. For example, an actor may answer a telephone as part of a scene.

Stage Positions

Actors and directors should be familiar with the various stage positions that best achieve visual focus. It is important for the stage to be set up in an appropriate manner so that the audience can focus on the action occurring on stage. Actors can use body positions to gain the audience's attention. A full front position or center stage automatically warrants the audience's attention. On stages that have multiple levels built into the set, an actor who stands at the highest level will hold the most visual focus. On a flat stage, the actor who stands farthest downstage, which is closest to the audience, will hold the most visual focus. If multiple actors are on stage they can be arranged in a triangular pattern with the actor at the apex of the triangle receiving the most visual focus. Actors can also be separated from the group by contrast. For example, if one actor on stage is standing while the rest are seated, the standing actor receives the visual focus.

Review Video: Understanding Action and Stage Directions
Visit mometrix.com/academy and enter code: 539974

Body Positions

Full front is a position in which the actor faces the audience exposing the entire front of the body. It is an open position that allows the actor to be fully seen and heard by the audience. Open positions are those in which the actor's face, at the very least is facing the audience. Quarter (¼) right and left positions are those in which the actor stands facing slightly left or right of the audience. Quarter positions are open positions. Quarter positions allow two actors to be on stage interacting with each other naturally while still allowing the audience to hear and see them. Left and right profiles are positions in which the actor exposes only one side of their face and body to the audience. Profiles are not open positions and drastically reduce the visibility of the actor to the audience. In between the profile and quarter positions are the three-quarter (¾) right and left positions. These are not quite profiles. Opposite of full front is the full back position. In full back position the actor faces away from the audience.

Staging Terms

A cross is a stage direction given by the director. It means the actor needs to move from one point on stage to another. For example, a director may instruct the actor to cross stage right. In a script, instructions to cross the stage are often shown by the letter "x." A direction to counter-cross is given in order to compensate for the cross of another actor. In order to retain a visual balance in a scene, the director may instruct one actor to cross stage right while instructing another actor to counter cross in order to avoid being blocked from view by the crosser. In general, if there are two actors on stage, each is of equal importance. If one actor steps farther away from the audience (or upstage), it causes an awkward interaction between the actors. The actor who has been upstaged must then turn his back to the audience in order to look as though he is naturally communicating with the other actor; however, this means the audience will not be able to hear the actor speaking. Upstaging should be avoided.

Preparing the Unit Set

Prior to using the unit set, each piece should be inspected for damage or instability. The pieces should be checked frequently for any signs of wear or damage, such as exposed nails, torn canvas, holes in the fabric, or exposed wood which might splinter. At the end of each show, any set pieces which were stood upon should be wiped down to avoid damage. Students must be taught that the unit set is extremely expensive and valuable, and should not be allowed to horseplay or jump on the set pieces (with the exception of blocked stage movements where applicable).

Safely Setting the Stage

Setting a stage is the process of constructing the scene that will take place, this includes moving props, changing lighting, moving and adjusting curtains, and making any changes that impact the appearance of the stage as needed in a scene. This begins with planning sets and drawing detailed scenes to scale, these drawings provide all crew with a detailed outline and better understanding of the needed outcome. To meet some settings needs, it may be necessary to build props which may require the use of cutting, fastening, clamping, and measuring tools. As such, wearing proper safety gear, like safety glasses and gloves, and appropriate attire, like close toed shoes and tying back long hair, is the first step in ensuring safety. Every power tool should have its own set of instructions and safety features that crew members need to familiarize themselves with before using. Because a stage is set multiple times during a production, there are some considerations to take regarding safety. Props, specifically furniture and large pieces, should be kept light where that is an option. When that is not an option, crew members need to be taught proper, safe lifting and moving techniques as they will be frequently and quickly moving these pieces between scenes.

Safely Striking the Stage

Striking is the deconstruction process of a set and occurs following the final performance. It is considered the most dangerous part of a production as the physical demands of this process carry an inherent risk, so it is crucial to follow safety procedures. Striking begins with the creation of a **strike plan** that outlines where and what type of deconstruction needs to occur and how many crew members it will require. After the plan has been created but before the strike occurs, a **strike training** will take place. The plan is shared and all safety information is reviewed during training. Personal protection equipment, like glasses, helmets, and gloves, need to be provided to the crew before beginning the strike. Understanding stage terminology will also ensure safety. **"Heads-up"** alerts crew members that something above them is moving or falling while **"clear"** alerts members that an object in the area is falling and they need to move. These cumulative actions help to ensure the safety of crew members as they strike the set and return the stage back to its original condition.

Backstage Procedures and Production Crews

Backstage Etiquette and Safety

Backstage, particularly when the lights are off, is the place where stage accidents or injuries are most likely to happen. Safety procedures such as using glow-in-the-dark gaff tape around designated prop areas can help actors and crew members avoid dangerous areas when the lights are out. All cast and crew should be taught backstage etiquette such as not running, avoiding horseplay, team carrying heavier items, and whispering when a show is in progress. Depending on the age of students, clear guidelines for not utilizing backstage spaces inappropriately must be discussed. Many high school programs choose to keep their curtains open and backstage lights on during rehearsals to avoid giving students dark and secluded areas for extended periods of time.

Properly Preparing the Set and Lighting Crew for Performances

Preparing lighting begins with a thorough reading of the script to determine production needs. The type and style of lighting to be used is determined by the setting and desired ambiance. While reading the script, a **cue list** is created. The cue list tells the crew what type of lighting to use, when to use it, and what effect it will create if applicable. This information will also be used to prepare a **lighting plan** to properly set the stage. The lighting plan lays out where the light sources need to come from, what type of lights to use, and how to use them to meet the needs outlined in the cue list. Using that plan, the crew will begin to construct the **lighting rigs**. This portion of set up requires the lights to be physically installed and manipulated, so it carries the risk of injury; therefore, it is vital to review safety precautions with the crew before beginning. Once the lights are set, the set designer continues the creative process to finalize the use of lights. Preparing the crew for curtain and fly rail operation use follows a similar process. **Curtain cues** are pulled from the script and tell the crew how and when to open and draw curtains. **Rail cues** signify when the fly rail system should be used to remove or place props from or onto the stage.

Stage Manager, Production Manager, Technical Director, and Production Crew

- **Stage Manager:** The stage manager is responsible for the people involved in a production. Some of the responsibilities include coordinating cast and crew schedules, scheduling rehearsals, coordinating and communicating between parties involved in the production, calling cues, and overseeing the show when performed live.
- **Production Manager:** Production managers work in a more typical managerial capacity. This can include budgeting, safety procedures, and general problem solving to prevent any issues that interfere with the production and a timely opening.
- **Technical Director:** Technical directors work to oversee all of the technical work done in a production. This includes lighting, sound, construction, carpentry, and general maintenance.
- **Production Crew:** The production crew is responsible for setting and striking the stage. They prepare and maintain equipment needed for performances. They oversee any moving components of the production, such as curtains, lights, props, or special effects.

Safety Practices and Procedures Related to Technical Theatre

Technical theatre is the components of a production that establish a setting and mood. It is also called **stagecraft**. Much of the preparation of technical theatre is physically involved, such as building sets, rigging lights, operating curtains, and moving large scene pieces. As such, safety practices and procedures should be established and reviewed with the crew to keep them safe.

Most common safety practices include wearing personal protection equipment, such as goggles, gloves, and closed-toe shoes, and ensuring no clothing or hair is loose as it may get caught in equipment. Ensuring exits are clear and easy to access at all times is necessary for the safety of all individuals. For large and heavy set pieces, the crew needs to ensure they are properly lifting using safe techniques and implementing assistive devices for moving. Individual tools, set pieces, and various pieces of equipment may have their own sets of instructions and safety procedures. These need to be reviewed by crew members and physical copies should be easy to access for anyone using them. Reminding the crew to stay alert at all times will help prevent injury by ensuring they remain aware of the risks that surround them.

Assembling a Production Crew

Assembling a production crew starts with establishing the needs of the production and creating roles that will fulfill those needs. This will include things like building set pieces, working lighting and curtains, and costume design. Those roles and expectations are then communicated with any interested parties, typically through theatre class periods, postings within the school building, or email blasts. Roles will vary in the level of time commitment required and if any prior theatre experience is necessary. With this information, the theatre teacher should begin connecting with students enrolled in the theatre class or interviewing interested students. During this time, the teacher should be as clear and direct as possible in outlining expectations. This will ensure that the students are aware of their commitments and the teacher will find someone ready to fill the role. Once students are selected for their roles, the crew can begin meeting as a whole to prepare for the production.

Teaching Proper Etiquette, Safety, and Backstage Techniques

Theatre crew plays a massive role in ensuring a production runs smoothly and is enjoyable for the audience as well as for the cast. As such, it is vital to ensure they have an understanding of proper etiquette, safety, and backstage techniques. Theatre etiquette encompasses the behaviors expected from the crew, such as speaking to one another and making requests respectfully, arriving on-time to rehearsals, adhering to deadlines, and general respect for all other parties involved in the production. The etiquette expectations should be clearly communicated to the crew as should consequences of not meeting these expectations. Having **"crew only" rehearsal** opportunities allow for intense crew training as well as time for the teacher to build rapport with the crew. These rehearsals serve as a time to ensure proper safety procedures are taught as well as an ample amount of time to practice any backstage techniques, like handling props, making changes and adjustments between scenes, and adjusting lighting and sounds. This again serves as an opportunity to outline what is expected and what happens if those expectations are not met. By working with crew only, the teacher also opens lines of communication that will make things run more smoothly.

Chapter Quiz

Ready to see how well you retained what you just read? Scan the QR code to go directly to the chapter quiz interface for this study guide. If you're using a computer, simply visit the online resources page at **mometrix.com/resources719/nystcetheater166** and click the Chapter Quizzes link.

Theater Tools, Media, and Techniques

Theatrical Lighting and Sound Production

LIGHTING

Lighting in theatre can be used in several ways. The most basic purpose of theatre lighting is to allow the audience to see what is happening on stage. Lighting is also useful for providing depth to the stage and actors. The use of highlights and shadows, called modeling, creates a three-dimensional effect. Lighting can serve an overall compositional purpose by helping to create a series of connected imagery that brings the director's interpretation to life. It can be used to give information about the setting of a play, pinpointing the time of day, the season and location. Light can also be used to focus the audience's attention on a particular element of the production or to create a mood for a play. The proper lighting can reflect the emotional content of a performance lending to a cohesive and balanced production.

ELEMENTS CONTROLLED BY LIGHTING DESIGNERS

Light has six primary qualities that can be controlled by lighting designers:

- Intensity is the light that is reflected by a performer and the background .
- Color is the color of the light reflected by the actor and background. It can be controlled through use of colored gels, lamp temperatures and dimmers.
- Direction, the angle of the light, determines the size and direction of shadows.
- Distribution is controlled by the type of lighting, the focus of the light, masking devices and the direction of the light source .
- Texture refers to the degree of diffusion or clarity in a light source. Texture is determined by the type of light, diffusion gels and screening devices.
- Movement refers to changes in intensity, direction, distribution, color and texture.

PROPERTIES OF LIGHT

Each function of stage lighting can be achieved in various ways through the manipulation of the properties of light. Visibility can be altered by the use of intensity, color and direction. Intensity and distribution determine the focus of stage lighting. Modeling is primarily achieved through the manipulation of light direction. Information, like visibility, can be achieved by the use of intensity, color and direction. For example, daytime scenes have brighter lighting than nighttime scenes. The mood of a play can be altered through use of the light properties of intensity, color, direction and distribution. The overall mood of a comedy is often best projected in warm, bright light while tragedies have darker lighting. The manipulation of all these functions and properties determines the success of the composite function of lighting, which serves to create a coherent production.

TYPES OF LIGHTS

- The **profile spot**, also called the ellipsoidal reflector spotlight, provides a hard-edged beam of light. Profile spots offer a beam that has a fixed size with a high intensity and very little stray light.
- **Templates** or **stencils** called gobos can be inserted into profile spots to cast a specific image or affect.
- The **Fresnel spot** offers a soft-edged beam with controllable size.
- **Soft-edged** lights like the Fresnel spot are used to light adjacent stage areas because the soft edges allow the lighting to overlap without creating any hard edges.

- The **pebble-convex** offers a semi-hard-edged beam. Like profile spots, pebble-convex lights have little or no stray light.
- The **par** is used when an intense and fixed beam of light is needed. Pars can be compared to the headlights of a car.
- The **floodlight** is used to flood a large area with light.

Profile spotlight: The profile spot works by reflecting a lamp's light and then passing the light through a gate. A plano-convex lens is used to focus the light and the gate has four shutters that can be moved in order to shape the light beam. Gate runners are built into the light to allow for irises and gobos to be inserted. Irises are devices that control the circular size of the light beam. Gobos are stencils that create patterns of light and shadow. For example, a gobo could be inserted to cast the image of a windowpane. The intensity of the light depends on the size of the beam, with narrow beams producing the highest intensity. The light can be flat-field or peak. Flat-field means that the light is evenly distributed throughout the beam. Peak refers to the higher concentration of light at the center of the beam. Profiles often have two lenses, one of which can be adjusted to control the size of the beam, while the other is adjusted to control the focus.

Floodlights: Floodlights are used to flood an area with light. There are three types of floodlights: evenly spread, bottom concentration and battens. Evenly spread floodlights provide light to a large area with every part of the beam emitting the same amount of light. Floodlights that are concentrated on the bottom emit a heavier light in the lower part of the beam, achieved by shaping the reflector part of the floodlight with an epitaxial lamp. Battens are created when floodlights are attached in long strips and used to light specific areas. Battens that are set up on the stage floor are called ground rows, those used on the front edge of the stage are called footlights and battens suspended from the ceiling are called border lights or magazine battens.

Terms Relating to Stage Lighting

- The **lighting structure**, which can include side lights, top lights and back lights, refers to the manner in which lights are set up to fall upon the stage and the actors.
- **Flat front light** is a lighting technique in which a beam is focused directly on an actor's face. Flat front light is often used to correct for key lighting, which can decrease the visibility of an actor's eyes. Using flat front light can correct this by making the actor's eyes more visible. Flat lighting can also be cast at a 45-degree angle for a more flattering look.
- **Key light** refers to the main source of lighting in a particular scene. Key lighting often creates unintentional areas of shadow, which are lit by fill lights.
- **Side lighting** involves lights that are set up on the sides of the stage above the actors' heads, allowing the actors to be seen when they are facing the sides of the stage.
- **Backlight**, top light and bottom light are all basic lighting structures. Backlights, positioned to shine down upon an actor or scene from above and behind the subject, are used to separate the actor from the background as they create an intense halo around the head and shoulders of the actor. Backlighting does not alter the faces of the actors, so various colored backlights can easily be used to create a mood on the stage.
- **Top lights**, also called downlights, are positioned directly above the subject, shining on protruding facial and body features, which provides a high contrast.
- **Bottom light** is also called uplight. Uplights are positioned in front of and beneath the subject. This is a rare technique because it is a very unnatural lighting angle. Footlights are considered types of uplights. Uplights can provide a very eerie effect, which you can picture by imagining what happens when someone shines a flashlight up from their chin, a common technique used while telling ghost stories around a campfire.

Sound Technicians' Tools

In the early days of theatre, sound was created by any means available. For example, the sound of thunder was simulated by rolling a cannonball down a narrow trench carved into the roof of a theatre. Now the sound of thunder can be created through use of digital sound equipment. Technicians have the ability to reproduce sounds made by things like doorbells and telephones. Technicians can also reinforce these sounds through use of amplification. The variety of technology available now allows for technicians to reproduce nearly any sound needed for a performance. Background music and actors' voices can all be controlled through use of speakers, microphones and soundboards. Sound quality is a crucial part of any theatre experience and a successful performance allows the audience to both see and hear the performance without distraction.

Editing and Video Installation

Montage, or editing, is probably the one discipline unique to film, video, and television. The timing, rhythm and progression of shots form the ultimate composition of the film. This procedure is one of the most critical elements of post-production and incorporates sound editing and mixing, as well as the design and execution of digital special effects.

In the case of a video installation, the method of presentation becomes critical. The work may be screened on a simple monitor, projected on a wall or other surface or incorporated into a larger sculptural installation. A video installation may also involve sound, with similar considerations to be made based on speaker design and placement, volume and tone.

Terms Relating to Lighting

- **A1-code** is the code used by the Lighting Industry Forum to identify the recommended usage of various lamps. A1 lamps are recommended for projection.
- An **advance bar** is a lighting bar that is set up downstage of the proscenium arch.
- An **aero** is a light with a tight beam that produces very intense light, originally used as an aircraft landing light.
- **ALD** stands for "Association of Lighting Designers."
- **Animation disc**: metal disc with slots that can be rotated in front of a lantern to give the effect of movement in the light.
- **Backlight**: light that comes from upstage or behind the actors.
- **Baffle**: material that is used to prevent light from spilling over from one area into another. It may also refer to a panel used in an auditorium to reduce the reflection of sound.
- **Ballyhoo**: the lighting effect produced when swinging a spot beam in a figure eight patter.
- **Barndoors**: hinged metal flaps that are attached to the front of Fresnel spotlights, which can be opened or closed to control the light beam.
- **Beamlight**: a flood lantern that uses a parabolic reflector to create a high-intensity parallel beam.
- **Bifocal spot**: a profile light that contains two sets of shutters. One set produces a hard-edged light; the other, a soft-edged light.
- **Birdie**: a low-volt light that can be used as uplighting or to conceal set pieces.
- **Black hole**: a part of the stage that was left unlit intentionally or accidentally.
- **Bleed through**: when lighting is slowly cross-faded from a scene occurring downstage to one occurring upstage; the two scenes are separated by a piece of gauze which can be lit to appear either opaque or invisible.
- **Bleeding**: when dimmers are not trimmed correctly, allowing the lantern to glow even when the dimmer control is at a minimum.

- **Blinders**: lamps that are set up around a stage facing the audience to prevent them from seeing backstage.
- **Blues**: used backstage as working lights; usually remain on even when blackouts occur to help actors and technicians see what they are doing.
- **Breakup**: abstract Gobo* that is used to provide a textured light with no distinctive pattern.
- **Chase**: repetitious sequence in which the lighting state is changed.
- **CID**, *compact iodide daylight*: a light with a high-intensity lamp that simulates the look of daylight.
- **Cleaners**: lights that are turned on in order to clean and set up a theatre venue.
- **CMY**: refers to the colors cyan, yellow and magenta, which are used to mix colors in moving lights.
- **Color call**: the list that specifies all of the colors that will be needed for a specific lighting plan.
- **Color filter**: piece of colored plastic that blocks passing of the light of any color but its own.
- **Additive color**: occurs when two beams of different colors are focused onto the same area.
- **Subtractive color**: occurs when two colors of gels are placed in front of a lantern.
- **Color temperature**: refers to warmness or coolness of lighting; high-color temperature lights appear whiter or cool.
- **Cross fade**: occurs when one lighting effect is brought up to replace the current lighting effect.
- **CSI**, *compact source iodide*: light used in followspots.
- **Cue light**: the system of giving actors and other staff cues by light.
- **DLC**, *digital light curtain*: a remote-controlled batten with color changers.
- **Dim out**: when lighting is reduced, but not completely blocked out, during scene changes.
- **Donut**: refers to a metal plate with a center hole that can be inserted into lanterns to sharpen focus.
- **Douser**: metal flag that can be moved to block a beam of light in order to eliminate the need to cut off electricity.
- **Effects projector**: a lantern that can project images such as clouds or rain.
- **ERS**: ellipsoidal reflector spotlight.
- **FBO**: fade to blackout.
- **Fill light**: light used to compensate for the shadows created by key lighting.
- **Flagging**: waving one's hand in and out of a beam of light in order to determine where it is focused on stage.
- **Focus chart**: the record created by the lighting designer that reveals the exact focus of each lantern in a rig.
- **Hitting your mark**: term used when an actor is standing in the correct spot according to the stage lighting.
- **Hot spot**: the brightest part of a light beam; certain lanterns have controls to eliminate hot spots.
- **House lights**: lights used in the auditorium, though they are not part of the actual play.
- **Iris**: the aperture device placed in a profile lantern to change the size of the light beam; common in followspots.
- **Key light**: the dominant source of light for a performance, the direction of which can change as the play progresses in order to simulate, for example, the rising and setting of the sun.
- **Kicker lights**: refers to lights that flank actors; can be used to enhance the three-dimensional look of things on stage.

- **Lamp tray**: part of a lantern upon which the lamp holder is set; can be hinged, removable or fixed.
- **Lantern**: This term is used very loosely to refer to any unit of light equipment.
- **Limelight**: a type of light no longer used but the term has been adapted into slang for being famous, "in the limelight."
- **Luminaire**: term used to refer to any type of lighting equipment.
- **Lux**: the level of illumination appearing on a surface.
- **Moon box**: gives the effect of a rising moon by using a shallow round box with low-wattage lamps covered by thin cloth.
- **Naturalism**: approach to lighting that requires lanterns be placed according to where light would occur in nature.
- **Neutral density filter**: light filter that can be used to decrease the intensity of light without altering its color.
- **Overlay**: the wider spot when there are two followspots on the same performer.
- **Parcan**: lantern that can produce an intense beam of light; ideal for special effects.
- **Pearl**: lamp with a frosted finish that serves to diffuse light; used when soft light is needed.
- **Perches**: lighting platforms located on sides of a stage behind the proscenium.
- **Pin spot**: luminaire used to focus a small tight beam of light onto a specific spot.
- **Scoop**: lamp mounted in a large ellipsoidal reflector; usually produces soft-edged circular beam of light and is used as a floodlight.
- **Silk**: light filter used to stretch light in a particular direction.
- **Throw**: refers to the distance between a light source and the person or item being lit.
- **Tilt**: refers to the up-and-down movement of a lantern.
- **Wash**: a lighting cover that blankets the whole stage in a certain type or color of light.
- **Yo-yo**: the device used by lighting technicians to remotely adjust a gobo while it is set in a lantern.

Terms Related to Scenery, Technical Elements, and Equipment

- An **A-D converter** is an analog-to-digital converter, used in computer soundcards. It converts a varying electrical signal into binary data.
- **Absorption** is a surface's ability to absorb sound.
- **Acoustics** refers to the behavior of sound in certain areas and usually depends upon the size and shape of a space, as well as the presence of any sound-absorbing materials.
- **Ambient noise** is the sound that exists in a room when no sound sources are present.
- **Ampere**, called "amps" are the units of measurement that refer to the electrical current passing through a circuit.
- An **Amplifier** is a piece of sound equipment that converts a low voltage signal into a higher current signal.
- **Array**: the loudspeakers that are used in a performance.
- **Artic**: an articulated lorry used to transport sets, costumes, props and technical equipment between venues.
- **ASM** is an acronym for Assistant Stage Manager.
- **Attribute**: the parameters of moving light that can be controlled, such as pan, tilt and gobos.
- **Backing**: either the piece of scenery that hides the technical areas or the money that is invested in a commercial production.
- **Battens**: pipes or pieces of wood from which a variety of production elements can be hung.
- **Bell board**: a live sound effects board that can play sound effects such as doorbells, ringing phones and sirens.

- **Blacks**: the clothing worn by stage management to visually minimize their presence on stage, or the drapes affixed to the set to hide technical equipment.
- **Book flat**: free standing piece of scenery that can be folded in half for quick scene changes.
- **Boom-arm**: mechanical structure which is mounted on a microphone to facilitate movement.
- **Border**: a piece of cloth used to mask lighting rigs or flown scenery from the audience.
- **Boss plate**: metal plate in stage floor that is used to bolt down scenery.
- **Breakaway**: a prop or a part of the set that is made to break upon impact.
- **Burnout**: a colored gel that has lost its color or has melted with use.
- **Cans**: headsets, earpieces and headphones used to communicate between technical departments.
- **Chain pocket-tab**: pocket sewed into the bottom of a cloth to weigh the cloth down.
- **Check**: refers to a smooth decrease in the level of light or sound.
- **CL**: the imaginary centerline running down the middle of the stage.
- **Clipping**: occurs when sound is distorted due to the amp's inability to handle the level of signal.
- **Back cloth**: fabric hung at rear of scene.
- **Floorcloth** fabric designating the acting area or a part of a set.
- **Frontcloth** fabric hung downstage to hide scene changes.
- **Starcloth**: usually black fabric with several small lamps sewn on to give the effect of a starry sky.
- **Crash box**: sealed metal box that contains glass or other breakable items that is thrown backstage to produce the sound of items being broken onstage.
- **Dead**: adjective describing an article of equipment or scenery that is no longer being used.
- **Dead room**: a room that dulls sound because of its thick sound absorbers.
- **Dip**: multiple meanings; small hidden trap door at stage level which contains electrical outlets; clear lacquer used to tint bulbs for lighting; lighting equipment that is set up at stage level.
- **Distortion**: occurs when sound equipment is overloaded.
- **Door flat**: a moveable wall with a working door that is used for scenery.
- **Dry run**: a technical rehearsal that usually does not involve actors.
- **Fade**: gradual increase or decrease in the level of light or sound.
- **False perspective**: design technique that makes the set appear larger than it really is.
- **False proscenium**: a canvas or flat panel placed onto a proscenium stage in order to decrease the size of the space to accommodate a small set.
- **False stage**: a stage floor laid for a production in which scenery may need to be moved from beneath the stage or in order to accommodate a revolving set.
- **Fills**: speakers used in addition to the main sound system to project sound into certain areas.
- **Fireplace flat**: a flat piece of scenery that contains a fireplace.
- **Fit up**: the initial assembly of stage hardware for a production, including setting up scenery.
- **Flipper**: a narrow flat of scenery that is attached by a hinge to a wider flat.
- **Forced perspective**: design technique that can be used to make items look larger or smaller by placing them at certain spots on the stage.
- **Haas effect**: psychoacoustic phenomenon, produced through experimentation with sound, which produces a 10-15 millisecond delay in sound, which allows the audience to remain focused on the actors and not become distracted by the delayed sound.
- **IATSE**, International Alliance of Theatrical Stage Employees: the union for stage employees.

- **Inset**: a small set that is arranged inside of a larger set.
- **Low smoke**: an effect produced when smoke is made to lie close to the floor; can be produced by chilling the smoke as it comes from smoke machine.
- **Marking out**: applying tape to the stage floor during rehearsal to identify the space upon which scenery will later be placed.
- **Maroon**: a pyrotechnic device that can create a loud explosive sound.
- **Masking**: material, neutral in color and used both to define a performance area and to hide technical areas.
- **Noise gate**: used to decrease background noise, maintaining a specific sound level by muting or increasing a signal in response to the noise level.
- **OP**: opposite prompt: refers to the side of the stage opposite of the side from which prompts are received.
- **Prompt book**: master copy of a script that details all of the actors' movements and technical cues; usually maintained by stage management.
- **Rider**: information sent to a venue by a theatrical company providing a detailed list of all of the technical requirements needed for a performance.
- **Scrim**: coarse gauzy fabric with several purposes, including scenery and lighting.
- **Show cloth**: a piece of material that contains the logo or title of a specific show; usually travels with a company for easy display in each venue.
- **Spike**: occurs when someone marks the position of a prop or a piece of the set on stage.
- **Stock scenery**: pieces of scenery that are kept in storage to be used throughout several performances.
- **Strike**: the disassembling of stage sets.
- **Thunder run**: a channel down which a cannonball can be run to simulate the sound of thunder.
- **Thunder sheet**: sheet of metal that can be shaken using two attached handles, or beaten, to simulate the sound of thunder.
- **Wagon stage**: complex scenery device in which bulky set items are positioned on sliding trucks, the width of the proscenium arch, mechanized to allow for quick scene changes.
- **Wipe**: refers to a single curtain that slides across a stage to hide it from view; may also be used as a backdrop or a part of the scenery.
- **Tab track**: the track that holds a moveable horizontal curtain that can be used to hide the stage or used as a backdrop for scenery.
- **Tabs**: curtains that are horizontally suspended to hide the stage area or are used as part of a backdrop.

Literary Elements in Drama

Styles of Drama

Classicism

Classicism is a theatrical style developed by French playwrights in the 17th century. In general, classicism places emphasis on society, reason and enlightenment. Classicism as a theatrical style incorporates the rules and traditions of ancient Greek and Roman theatre, embodying Aristotle's theories regarding the unity of time, place and action.

Neo-Classicism

Neoclassicism is a product of the 18th century. Neoclassicism, as a theatrical style, is characterized by extravagant costumes and elaborate scenery with stories that involve a high degree of melodrama. Neoclassic theatre has clearly defined genres of either tragedy or comedy.

Elizabethan

Elizabethan theatre is characterized by a high number of characters, several subplots that eventually merge and a varied mixture of emotion.

Restoration

Restoration drama, also known as the comedy of manners, is characterized by witty dialogue with themes of virtue and honor. Restoration theatre also featured plots involving the sexual behavior of sophisticated society.

Romanticism

Romanticism was the dominant style from 1750 to 1800. Romanticism is characterized by mankind's unfaltering trust in the kindness of nature. Reason was regarded as secondary to instinct and logic was forsaken for emotion. Romantic ideals encouraged the idea that a simple life was the most desirable kind. Romanticism allowed for the glorification of past civilizations, especially that of the Greeks. It also boasted the merit of the natural man in a primitive setting such as Native Americans. Romantic ideals encouraged the elimination of social classes and the heightened sense of detail. Romanticism fused comic and tragic styles into a unified form of drama that favored the individual actor above the type actor. Romanticism also favored abstraction and idealism. Romantic dramas had a tendency to use special effects because the style focused on visual appeal.

Realism

The ideology of realism was based on science and technology, suggesting that science could solve the problems of humanity. Realism stressed that truth was that which could be felt by the five senses and was characterized by contemporary settings and periods. The themes of realist drama were common to everyday people.

Naturalism

Naturalism, a branch of realism, was developed as a result of the work of Charles Darwin. Darwin's theories on evolution materialized into a form of drama with a prevailing pessimistic attitude in which there was no climax.

Expressionist

The goal of expressionist theatre was to express raw emotion, not to teach, entertain or duplicate reality. Expressionism is characterized by highly exaggerated movements and voice techniques to express the emotion of the characters. Expressionism also tends to dramatize the struggles and spiritual nature of protagonists as well as the struggles between differing social classes.

Absurdist

Absurdist drama is characterized by a lack of realistic characters, an ambiguous concept of time and a vague attempt to define the setting.

Types of Plays

Chronicle Plays

Chronicle plays are historical dramas based on English history written primarily during the Elizabethan and Jacobean periods. The source of many of these plays was Holinshed's "Chronicles of England, Scotland, and Ireland", thus the title "Chronicle Plays".

Mystery Plays

Mystery Plays are dramatic works based on the Bible. These dramas were usually produced by local trade guilds for the pleasure of their villages. They were presented in cycles that sometimes dramatized the entire New and Old Testaments. Mystery plays were performed in England, France, Spain, and Italy, among other countries. Passion plays are specialized mystery plays based on the passion of Christ.

Heroic Dramas

Heroic Dramas featured heroes of epic deeds. Usually written in blank verse or heroic couplets, these plays reached the apex of their popularity during the Restoration period.

Interludes

Interlude refers to a very short form of drama sometimes performed between courses of a banquet but also the term came to refer to any kind of musical or dramatic entertainment. These were usually performed for private parties and fell out of favor with the opening of public venues. Their popularity peaked in 16th century England.

Nos

No is a form of traditional Japanese theatre that use music, dance, and poetry. They make no claim to be realistic, rather creating a serene and peaceful mood through spectacle and imagery. No are based on eastern religions, reflecting themes from Hinduism and Buddhism. The plays have a fixed repertory that has been constant since the 1500's. William Butler Yeats adapted No for western audiences in a series of short plays. They remain popular with drama critics and certain classes of Japanese.

Problem Plays

Problem plays focus on social problems and movements. Alexander Dumas, son of the great French novelist, wrote a series of short plays attacking the ills of society. The early 19th century was the heyday of problem plays. Henrik Ibsen is perhaps the most celebrated playwright of problem plays, particularly with his treatment of women's rights in "The Doll House". Lillian Hellman and Arthur Miller have both written popular problem plays in the 20th century.

The term "problem plays" is used in a different context by Shakespearean scholars. These critics use the term for plays that have caused interpretation problems for audiences. Plays such as "All's Well That Ends Well", "Troilus and Cressida", and "Measure for Measure" lend themselves to various interpretations and pose literary problems for students of the bard.

Farce

A farce is a dramatic comedy that is full of action, escapades of characters always on the brink of disaster, and full of stereotypical characters filling stock roles. The farce is one of the oldest forms of comedy, found in folk plays, Greek drama, the Renaissance and modern theatre. The 'Bedroom farce' is a special type of comedy based on the foibles of attempted seductions. It continues to be popular in modern theatre, notably in the work of Alan Ayckbourn. The theater of the absurd uses farce to represent the essential meaninglessness and chaos of life. Specialized forms of this are tragic farce, which combines farce with tragedy. Farce is perhaps best known by the public through silent films, where Charlie Chaplin, the Keystone Cops and many other slapstick comedians made film an excellent example of farce enjoyed by a wide audience.

Aristotle's Six Elements of Drama

Aristotle identified six elements that define drama:

- Plot refers to the story elements of a play, including the arrangement of the events that take place in the story.
- Character refers to the physical, mental or emotional qualities demonstrated by actors allowing the audience to see them as unique individuals.
- Diction refers to the language employed by the playwright.
- Idea or Thought is defined as the theme that the author is attempting to convey to the audience.
- Spectacle refers to the visual elements of a play. These include make-up, costumes and sets.
- Sound or Song refers to the actual music used in a play as well as all other auditory devices, which can include the rhythm of spoken lines and sound effects. Diction refers to the language of the play. The language is a crucial element, as it reveals both overt and subtle information about characters and situations in a play.

These six elements are, according to Aristotle, what every drama has in common. Modern critics often also refer to all of the elements of plot, character, and dialog as one single element, also called plot.

Action

Modern critics have elaborated upon these elements. Aristotle's original element of action is comprised of eight sub-elements: exposition, problem, point of attack, foreshadowing, complications, crises, climax, and denouement. Exposition provides the audience with information about the time period, setting, characters, relationships and events of the play. The problem is the event that sets the plot in motion. The point of attack is the way the author presents the problem. The author may have the problem occur before or after the main character is introduced. Foreshadowing refers to the clues planted by the writer that will result in a believable finish. Complication is the event that occurs after the problem is introduced. The complication is the obstacle that could prevent the character from achieving a goal. The crisis is the point where the character must make a crucial decision or undergo a significant event. The height of the crisis is the climax, which represents the peak of the entire plot. The story finally concludes with the denouement.

Key Aspects of Drama

Theme

Ideas or concepts given sustained attention in a drama highlight the major themes of the work. Often the title of the play reflects themes to be presented.

Argument

Some works are really expositions of arguments and points that the author wants to make. Arguments and themes are given dramatic force through the form in which they are expressed. This could be action, speech, or narration.

Patterns of Imagery

These include the use of symbols and keywords. These are recurring motifs that form themes and plot development together. Some plays focus on a particular image. Symbols are subtle devices used by authors for a variety of reasons, and they are usually a key to the major themes of the drama. Symbols may change as the play progresses, and these changes are important in plotting and action. Some key words are used as symbols and are repeated and emphasized to enrich the material. These keywords may be tied to one character or shared by many.

Progression of a Dramatic Plot

When studying dramatic works, significant events in the story should be recognized. Major shifts or reversals in the plot, and subsequent action should be followed carefully. Aristotle's "Poetics" described a typical progression pattern of a plot as follows:

1. Exposition
2. Complication
3. Reversal
4. Recognition
5. Resolution

This progression is still valid today as we study and analyze plots. The plot may follow the pattern of comedy (ending with a celebration), or tragedy (ending with death). The plot may be explained through dialogue, stage action, and off-stage events or by a chorus. While plots of well known plays are easily understood and analyzed, more esoteric drama requires more careful attention to the plot's complexities.

Advancing the Plot

Authors use many devices to maintain interest and advance the plot. Among these are building tension between characters, creating difficult situations that cannot easily be resolved, and highlighting conflict and romance. Often authors choose not to reveal some information that increases tension. Action is the physical events in a play. Action can be important or have little dramatic impact. Some plays depend on spectacles rather than dialogue to emphasize plot and characters. Staging is an important element in the action of a drama. The play may be written for a particular acting space, necessary for the action employed. The theatre the play was written to be performed in often dictates the scope of action in the work. A work requiring lavish spectacles is usually not written for small theatres. Adaptations may be made in specific productions to allow more or less" action space".

Knowledge of Characters

In order to understand a dramatic work, detailed knowledge of major characters is essential. Details of their past, motivations for their actions, fatal flaws, romantic relationships, antagonistic characters, and historical context all weave a tapestry of characters that fill out a drama's skeleton. It is vital to distinguish between major characters, who are central to the drama and minor ones who are only functional. The extent to which each character is developed is a good clue in identifying major and minor personae. Details of the relationships between characters often are an excellent guide to plot development and resolution. Who loves whom, who hates whom, who are allied, who are enemies, and the implications of these tangled webs form the structure of plot and drama. Of the many possible relationships in a play, only a few will be crucial. These should be identified and followed closely.

Review Video: Determining Relationships in a Story
Visit mometrix.com/academy and enter code: 929925

Speech and Dialogue

Analysis of speech and dialogue is important in the critical study of drama. Some playwrights use speech to develop their characters. Speeches may be long or short, and written in as normal prose or blank verse. Some characters have a unique way of speaking which illuminates aspects of the drama. Emphasis and tone are both important, as well. Does the author make clear the tone in which lines are to be spoken, or is this open to interpretation? Sometimes there are various possibilities in tone with regard to delivering lines.

Asides and Soliloquies

Asides and **soliloquies** can be important in plot and character development. Asides indicate that not all characters are privy to the lines. This may be a method of advancing or explaining the plot in a subtle manner. Soliloquies are opportunities for character development, plot enhancement, and to give insight to characters' motives, feelings, and emotions. Careful study of these elements provides a reader with an abundance of clues to the major themes and plot of the work.

Apostrophe and Soliloquy

Apostrophe occurs when a character addresses an abstract idea or a persona not present in the scene. This differs from a soliloquy where a character seems to be speaking to himself or thinking out loud. The soliloquy was used extensively in English Renaissance drama and made popular by Shakespeare in his dramatic works. The soliloquy has evolved into interior monologues in fiction where the musings of a character are used to develop depth and advance plots. Apostrophe and soliloquy are often confused, and it should be remembered that a soliloquy occurs when there is only one character on the stage, while in apostrophe there may be other characters in the scene but not addressed.

Antistrophe

Antistrophe is a device in Greek drama where the chorus responds to a previous stanza of verse. Antistrophe is rarely seen today outside of the production of classical Greek drama.

Agony

Agony is the Greek word for struggle or conflict. As used in classical Greek drama, it indicates a portion of the play in which two characters engage in a heated argument or debate. Each of the characters is supported in their arguments by a part of the Greek chorus. The agony is a device used extensively in both comedies and tragedies. It is often the part of Greek drama when climaxes of the plot unfold. The opposing characters usually represent conflicting themes or ideas in the drama. In tragedies the agony is sometimes followed by the death or exile of the protagonist.

In modern literature the term is used in literary criticism to denote a competitive battle. Harold Bloom used the term as an element in literary history in terms of the conflict between a major poet and his or her predecessor whom the poet feels he must displace.

Chorus

Utilized in Greek drama, the **chorus** is a group of actors who furnish a commentary on the play as it unfolds. The chorus in Greek drama probably evolved from the choral tradition of musical productions. Traditionally, the chorus speaks for society rather than any character in the play. This means the chorus is the objective observer of the dramatic action. Shakespeare occasionally used the chorus in some of his plays. Henry V and Romeo and Juliet are examples of this. In musical dramas, the term refers to a group of singers and dancers who play an important part of the production. Modern drama usually does not employ a chorus, although it was used in T.S. Eliot's play "Murder in the Cathedral" in 1935. The chorus in modern musical theatre often acts a collective actor that adds to the spectacle of the production.

BRAINSTORMING

Brainstorming is a technique used frequently in business, industry, science, and engineering. It is accomplished by tossing out ideas, usually with several other people, in order to find a fresh approach or a creative way to approach a subject. This can be accomplished by an individual by simply free-associating about a topic. Sitting with paper and pen, every thought about the subject is written down in a word or phrase. This is done without analytical thinking, just recording what arises in the mind about the topic. The list is then read over carefully several times. The writer looks for patterns, repetitions, clusters of ideas, or a recurring theme. Although brainstorming can be done individually, it works best when several people are involved. Three to five people is ideal. This allows an exchange of ideas, points of view, and often results in fresh ideas or approaches.

FREEWRITING

Freewriting is a form of brainstorming in a structured way. The method involves exploring a topic by writing about it for a certain period of time without stopping. A writer sets a time limit and begins writing in complete sentences everything that comes to mind about the topic. Writing continues without interruption until the set period expires. When time expires, read carefully everything that has been written down. Much of it may make little or no sense, but insights and observations may emerge that the free writer did not know existed in his mind. Writing has a unique quality about it of jogging loose ideas, and seeing a word or idea appear may trigger others. Freewriting usually results in a fuller expression of ideas than brainstorming, because thoughts and associations are written in a more comprehensive manner. Both techniques can be used to complement one another and can yield much different results.

POETRY

FIGURATIVE LANGUAGE

Poetry is a genre in which language is used in all its variations and embellishments to convey a sense, mood, or feeling the poet deems important. Poetry uses elaborate linguistic constructions to explain the world in creative ways. Poetry manipulates language itself to convey impressions in new and innovative constructions. It makes extensive use of figurative devices such as conceits, similes, metaphors and many more to express things in fresh ways. These devices will be treated separately later. Together, poets use **figurative language** to suggest rather than give direct meanings. This language provides a creative experience for the reader who is asked to understand meaning in unconventional terms. Poets relish the opportunities to express themselves in creative and unusual words. Figurative language provides both poet and reader an opportunity for unique expression and understanding. Emotions, feelings, and moods are invoked by the skillful use of figurative language.

HYPERBOLE

Hyperbole is a figure of speech that uses extreme exaggeration for dramatic effect. It usually functions to compare and is used quite often in romantic works. Love poetry is an example of a subgenre that fosters the use of hyperbole. Hyperbole may also be used in a farcical manner for comic effect.

Personification

Personification is another figure of speech, which attributes human qualities to an inanimate object or abstract entity. Personification helps us to use our self-knowledge and extrapolate it to understand abstract concepts, forces of nature, and common events. Personification is sometimes achieved by similes or analogies to strengthen the imagery.

Foreshadowing

Foreshadowing uses hints in a narrative to let the audience anticipate future events in the plot. Foreshadowing can be indicated by a number of literary devices and figures of speech, as well as through dialogue between characters. In Ibsen's play "Hedda Gabler", Hedda plays with a gun early in the play, which foreshadows her eventual suicide. In Shakespeare's "Macbeth", the three witches in the opening scene foreshadow horrific events to come. Examples abound in all forms of literature but are perhaps most evident in drama.

Allusions

An **allusion** is a reference within a text to some person, place, or event outside the text. Allusions that refer to events more or less contemporary with the text are called topical allusions. Those referring to specific persons are called personal allusions. An example of personal allusion is William Butler Yeats' reference to "golden thighed Pythagoras" in his poem "Among School Children". Allusions may be used to summarize an important idea or point out a contrast between contemporary life and a heroic past. An example of this would be James Joyce's classical parallels in "Ulysses" in which heroic deeds in the "Odyssey" are implicitly compared to the banal aspects of everyday life in Dublin. Allusions may also be used to summarize an important idea such as the concluding line from "King Kong", "It was beauty killed the beast". A writer may use allusions as literary devices to achieve a number of dramatic effects as noted above.

Style of Literature

In literature, **style** is a particular manner of using language to narrate a story, develop a dramatic mood, or evoke a mood. Style can also refer to a period of literary history or to an individual writer.

Tone

Tone refers to the attitude expressed about the subject through the author. This expression is communicated by language, character development, plotting, and the creation of attitudes about the subject. Mood is sometimes mistaken for tone, but the two have important differences. Mood is generally understood to be the feeling the work provokes in the audience. Although this can sometimes be identical to tone, they are often quite different.

Diction

Diction is the choice of language in a literary work. Diction may be formal, colloquial, or slang. The use of diction to set a tone for the work is meant to induce a mood in the audience. Slang is used commonly in modern fiction while formal and colloquial diction are used for specific effects.

Characters

A **protagonist** is the central character in a play or story. The character opposing the protagonist is called the **antagonist**. Either may be the hero or villain of a drama or work of fiction. In modern literature the protagonist-antagonist struggle is often represented as an internal conflict in one individual. Freudian thought has had a great influence on this inward battle of psychological forces in a person. The **hero** or **heroine** is also the major figure in a literary work. The term may be used instead of protagonist. Finally, the villain is the major evil character in a literary work. Usually the **villain** opposes the protagonist but sometimes is the protagonist of a work. The roles of heroes and villains are exaggerated in melodrama and often seen in early films. The conflict in these cases usually involves a "**fair damsel**". Modern literature usually reflects a more **mixed character**, with both qualities present in a character.

Plot Development

Climax

A **climax** occurs when a state of tension in a literary work reaches its peak, usually with a resolution of some kind. There may be many or only one climax in a work, depending on the plotting and length of the story. A climax is usually preceded by an increasing level of tension, usually between the protagonist and antagonist. The climax may take the form of action, speech, or symbolism.

Anticlimax

An **anticlimax** occurs in fiction or drama when a critical point in the work is resolved and the dramatic tension recedes. The term can be used negatively if it refers to a weakness in a drama or story. Sometimes an anticlimax is used to enhance a scene or serve as a respite from a period of action.

Closure

Closure is the modification of the structure of a work, which makes absence of further development unlikely. It creates the expectation of nothing and leaves the reader or audience satisfied that the plot development is over. Closure often has a dramatic force of its own and sometimes is the final climax.

Review Video: How to Make a Story Map
Visit mometrix.com/academy and enter code: 261719

Syllogism

Deductive reasoning is constructed in a three-step method called a **syllogism**. The three steps are the major premise, the minor premise, and the conclusion. The major premise is a generalization, and the minor premise is a specific case. The conclusion is deduced from applying the generalization to the specific case. Deductive arguments fail if either the major or minor premise is not true, or if the conclusion does not logically follow from the premises. This means a deductive argument must stand on valid, verifiable premises, and the conclusion is a logical result of the premises.

Straw Man Fallacy

The "**straw man**" fallacy consists of an oversimplification or distortion of opposing views. This fallacy is one of the most obvious and easily uncovered since it relies on gross distortions. The name comes from a side setting up a position so weak (the straw man) that is easily refuted.

Actor vs. Dramatist

The dramatist must make sure that the venue for which he is writing will be physically able to handle the demands of his play. The dramatist must also be mindful of the audience for which he is writing as well as the abilities of the actors who will be portraying the characters he creates. The ability of the actor is crucial to the creation of a character because an actor can impose his or her own personality onto a character created by a dramatist. Some dramatists tend to write about characters in the abstract, creating characters from their imagination. Some dramatists create characters based on actual people. Ancient dramatists created characters for the actor who would play the role and both Shakespeare's and Moliere's works were influenced by the actors for whom they were writing. The actor whom the dramatist has in mind when creating a character has a great impact on the creation of that character.

Deus ex Machine

The term **deus ex machine** is Latin for "God out of a machine." The term originated in Greek tragedy where an actor playing the role of God was lowered onto the stage by some mechanical device. In modern usage, the term refers to a character or event that is suddenly introduced into a work of fiction in order to help resolve some problem or dilemma.

Character Design

Character Analysis

In order to play the part of any character, an actor should undergo a character analysis, which is the process by which the actor learns about the unique elements that make up the character. A character can consist of vocal patterns, physical appearances, mannerisms, feelings, prejudices, aspirations, emotions and goals. The actor must study or think about all of these elements and the degree to which each of these elements are integrated within the character. The actor should try to understand the character's relationship with others, their psychological thought process, their weaknesses and strengths, their sense of morality and their history. The actor must also consider the character's place in the story and how or if the character will be changed by the events of the story.

Character Development

Externals

Externals refer to the elements that an actor can use in their environment to aid in creating specific characters. An external can be a costume, a vocal change, makeup or a set of mannerisms. For many actors, externals are the primary tools used to create a character. By dressing or speaking the way a character would, the actor can begin to relate to the feelings that the character would experience. Using externals to create a character is a method called "outside-in." This means that the actor uses outside elements to cause internal changes. In order to be a character actor, one must be able to shed the restrictions of an everyday persona. They must be able to essentially create a blank slate upon which the new character can be created.

Auguste Character

The **auguste character**-type is often an anarchist, a joker, or a fool. He is clever and has much lower status than the whiteface. Classically, the whiteface character instructs the auguste character to perform his bidding. The auguste has a hard time performing a given task, which leads to funny situations. Sometimes the auguste plays the role of an anarchist and purposefully has trouble following the whiteface's directions. Sometimes the auguste is confused or is foolish and is screwing up less deliberately.

The Contra-Auguste

The **contra-auguste** plays the role of the mediator between the whiteface character and the auguste character. He has a lower status than the whiteface but a higher status than the auguste. He aspires to be more like the whiteface and often mimics everything the whiteface does to try to gain approval. The contra-auguste character is often instructed by the whiteface to correct the auguste when he is doing something wrong.

Analyzing Characters

There are three types of objectives: objective, super-objective and sub-objective. The objective in the most general sense is the character's goal. In order to best analyze a character, one must be able to interpret what the script says directly and, even more importantly, what it says indirectly. One should be able to infer information about the character being analyzed from the choices the character makes, the relationships the character has and what other characters say and think about the character being analyzed. The basic objective is the character's goal in each scene. When analyzing a character, one should read the script with the intention of discovering what the character wants to accomplish in each scene. The super-objective is the character's goal for the whole play. It may also be called the spine or through line. The sub-objectives are small changes in a scene involving mood, subject and intention. Each of these objectives should be identified when analyzing a character.

Subtext

According to teacher, director and writer Robert Cohen, acting is the process of effectively interpreting and conveying the **subtext** in relationships between characters. He created the term "relacom" to refer to the communication in a relationship. When analyzing a character one should consider the overt characterization as well as the subtle characterization that is inferred from a character's body language, motives and interaction with other characters. It is important to understand what a character says but is just as important to understand the way it is said. The manner in which a character says things conveys the underlying meaning of the thoughts and actions behind the dialogue. Subtext is an important part of understanding a character, as it can define the identity of a character or clarify a relationship with another character. Subtext is often the key in developing an effective and believable character.

Chapter Quiz

Ready to see how well you retained what you just read? Scan the QR code to go directly to the chapter quiz interface for this study guide. If you're using a computer, simply visit the online resources page at **mometrix.com/resources719/nystcetheater166** and click the Chapter Quizzes link.

Theatre and Culture

Egyptian Passion Plays

One of the earliest preserved documents attesting to the existence of dramatic productions is a stone tablet from 2000 B.C. The tablet contains a description of the roles played by the Egyptian king Ikhernofret. The ancient productions are believed to resemble today's passion plays and served as a means to communicate the suffering and successes of a particular deity. Like modern passion plays, the ancient forms showed the trials faced by the god and ended with the resurrection of the god. Egyptian passion plays generally centered around the central god figure of Osiris, whose legend claims that he was murdered by his brother, but later resurrected. Osiris is often seen as the god who rules over the underworld. Records indicate that passion plays depicting the life of Osiris occurred annually in the cities of Abydos and Heliopolis.

Origin of Comedy

According to Aristotle, comedy was first introduced in a performance or festival called komos. Komos was an ancient Greek ritual in which a group of drunken males danced and sang, often in a procession, while carrying a large phallus. The phallic symbol was a tribute to the god Phales, believed to be the companion of Bacchus, the god of wine. Greek celebrations often ended with a group of young males parading in the city streets with torches in hand. Members of the group, called comoedus, were led in song by a flute- or lyre-player. The activity was known as a comus or komos. Aristotle further claimed that these events could be traced back to the Greek cities of Megaris and Sicyon. Aristotle supported this theory on the origins of comedy by stating that the first comic poet, Susarion, was an inhabitant of a town very near Megaris.

Origin of Tragedy

According to Aristotle, tragedy can be traced to the Greek songs called **dithyrambs**, which were sung in honor of the fertility god Dionysus. Greek men would dance while wearing costumes of goatskins in order to impersonate satyrs, as these were the constant companions of Dionysus. The song sung by these men was called a **tragoedia**, which means "goat-song" in Greek. This ritual was expanded upon by the addition of a central male figure to which the songs were addressed. The central male figure would answer questions sung to him by the surrounding circle males or chorus. The word chorus is derived from the Greek word "choros," which meant to dance in a circle. There are many differing views on the exact origin of the tragedy, but the above describes the basic consensus among scholars.

William Ridgeway's Theory

In 1904, the interpretation of Aristotle's origins of tragedy came into question. Scholars began to question Aristotle's theory as well as modern man's interpretation of this theory. William Ridgeway, a writer and scholar, published a book in which he presented the theory that tragedy originated not from the worship of the god Dionysus but from the worship of the dead. This completely changed the geographical origins of Aristotle's theory because the worship of the dead was much more widespread. Ridgeway believed that the cult of Dionysus was introduced to the city of Sicyon by the statesman Cleisthenes. Ridgeway further explained that Dionysus was worshipped as a hero among the Greeks because he was a mortal man who became a saint and was elevated to god-like status. Ridgeway supported his theory by offering as evidence the fact that Dionysus, like most dead kings of the time, had an oracle within his temple. Based on this knowledge, the worship of Dionysus is actually the worship of the dead, making both Aristotle and Ridgeway's theories correct.

Elements of Tragedy

A **tragedy** is a play in which a heroic character, through unfortunate circumstances, experiences a downfall. The unfortunate circumstances are usually orchestrated by the gods as a punishment for the sin of hubris, the sin of pride. It is common for the hero to have a desire to attain some type of power that would liken them to a god. The constraints of mortality would not allow a human to achieve a goal or attain a power that is reserved for gods. The hero in a tragedy is usually depicted as a likeable but flawed character who begins the tragedy as an ignorant being but ends the tragedy as an enlightened being. The events that unfold are such that they change the hero's life and manner of thinking. The hero is not required to die to learn his lesson but must go through a major change or enlightenment as the tragedy progresses.

Characteristics of Greek Comedy

Old Greek Comedy

The year of 450 B.C. marks the approximate start of **Old Comedy**, which evolved from the celebrations of the god Dionysus. Old Comedy was best known for its crude language and lack of restriction. Dramatists of Old Comedy were allowed to exercise poetic license to its fullest extent. It was common for the actors to verbally attack, ridicule and defame a well-known person who was generally disliked by the populace of Greece. Old Comedy served both as a source of entertainment and as a front for political campaigns. In order to best understand plays written in the time of Old Comedy, modern readers should take time to study the political climate of the time period in which the work was written. Although Old Comedy differed from Greek tragedies, the two also shared some attributes, such as the vital role of the chorus. Unlike the tragic plays of that time, Old Comedy did not use myths and legends as a basis for plot.

Middle Greek Comedy

Middle Comedy was the dominant form of Greek comedy from the end of the fifth century to the middle of the fourth century B.C. Middle Comedy differed from its predecessor in that it lacked the chorus. This was the first time the importance of the chorus was diminished in theatre. Prior to Middle Comedy, Old Comedy and tragedy had emphasized the role of the chorus. Unlike Old Comedy, Middle Comedy ceased to impersonate public characters on stage, diminishing the use of theatre as a political outlet. The focus of Middle Comedy shifted to fictional characters rather than current or historical figures. Middle Comedy introduced the comic figure of the sharp-tongued cook, present in many Greek plays.

New Greek Comedy

New Comedy was the genre that ruled the Greek stage from the late fourth century through 260 B.C. New Comedy was largely focused on the idea of unrequited or unattainable love and introduced the character of the mercenary soldier returning home from war. This form had no characters likened to public figures or heroes. Rather, the characters of New Comedy were common people who faced everyday problems. This new genre completely eliminated the chorus and was received well by audiences because the nature of its plays involved universal themes. The use of these common themes allowed for New Comedy to translate well in other geographic regions and it subsequently spread to Rome, Italy and to England. This ancient form of New Comedy was the foundation for the comic forms used in theatre and television today.

Ancient Athenian Drama

Athenian drama was seen as not only a source of entertainment but also as a religious celebration. The religious connection was a result of the fact that Athenian plays were performed only twice a year, usually during the two Dionysian festivals. Since the entertainment of the masses was considered a governmental duty, theatrical productions of ancient Athens were managed by the state. The state chose playwrights and actors while the wealthy upper-class citizens footed the bill. Plays were performed from morning to night during several days of the festivals. Generally, the performances were contests in which the winning poet was given a prize by the state. Almost every Athenian citizen would attend these productions and the twenty-thousand plus capacity of the theatre ensured that everyone could attend. The poets and playwrights chosen by the state received the great privilege of being heard by the entirety of Athens and it for this reason that these ancient artists had such a great impact on the manner in which we now view those times.

Origins of Satire

While most ancient forms of theatre are credited to the Greeks, **satire** was the invention of the Romans. The Roman satire was a tool used to criticize the current social situation. Roman satire took one of two forms: **Menippean** or **verse**. Menippean satire was named for its originator, Greek cynic Mennipus and is characterized by a rhapsodic blending of prose and verse that ridiculed various social characters. Seneca's work entitled The Apocolocyntosis is an example of the Menippean satire. Verse satire, created by Lucilius but most readily seen in the works of Horace, was generally composed in epic meter. The Roman satire bore a similarity to the Greek form of Old Comedy in that both were a means of attacking the injustices perpetuated by the political climate of the time.

Satyr Plays of the Early Greeks

Pratinus is recognized as the first writer of the Greek **satyr play**. Satyrs were the half-man, half-goat companions of the god Dionysus. In the early Greek plays, a group of males wearing goat costumes danced and sang in an act of worship directed towards the god Dionysus. These groups of goat-skinned dancers were impersonating satyrs and evolved into what became known as the chorus in many Greek tragedies. The chorus of satyrs, generally prone to merriment, were not appropriate accompaniment for the more serious Greek tragedies, so their role was increasingly diminished over time. In order to preserve the fun-natured spirit of the satyr chorus, Pratinus began to compose short plays in which this group took center stage. Athenian theatre became organized into tetralogies, compilations of three tragedies followed by one satiric piece. The purpose of including the satyr form was to allow the audience to recover from the serious nature of the tragedy by enjoying the more light-hearted jests of the satyr chorus.

Preservation of Greek Plays

It was the responsibility of the Athenian archons, or magistrates, to maintain records of Greek productions. They recorded names of the upper-class citizens who financed the productions, the poets, actors, plays and contest winners. These records were later published by Aristotle. Athenians had an insatiable appetite for theatre, as their normal viewings were limited to only a few days of the year. In order to satisfy the need for theatre during the off-season, many of the great plays of that time were rewritten by people known as adapters. To preserve the integrity of the original work, the law required that the distribution of any copy of an original work had to be recorded by a public secretary. The library at Alexandria holds copies of various tragic and satyr plays. The most common of the ancient Greek plays seen today are those that were preserved for use in educational institutions of the Middle Ages, including the works of Aeschylus, Sophocles, Euripides and Aristophanes.

Contributions to Theatre

Aeschylus, Sophocles and Euripides

Aeschylus, Sophocles and Euripides are considered the most famous Greek tragedians. Aeschylus is most noted for his trilogy called The Oresteia, which is comprised of Agamemnon, The Libation

Bearers, and The Eumenides. Aeschylus became known as the father of Greek tragedy, since he pre-dated both Sophocles and Euripides. According to Aristotle, Aeschylus was responsible for changing the ancient form of the tragedy by adding a second actor, which diminished the participation of the chorus and focused on the dialogue. Sophocles, known for his work Oedipus the King, heightened the tragic form by adding a third actor and downsizing the chorus to fewer than fifteen members. Euripides is known for several plays, including The Bacchae and Medea.

Position of Actor

Profession

In the plays of ancient Greece, there were two distinct roles: an actor and chorus members. Chorus members were selected by a group called the **choregus**, while actors were chosen by the state. The title of "actor" only applied to the person in the play with the most prominent dialogue. Early Greek plays featured only one actor with the number increasing to three in the later years. While only a limited number were called actors, several characters were present in plays, most of whom were silent or spoke only a few words. Before Aeschylus, the profession of actor was not distinct from that of poet because poets generally performed as actors. This distinction came about when Aeschylus introduced the second actor, meaning someone other than the poet was required to play a role in the production. In the early Athenian contests, only the poets received awards for their playwriting skills, but by the fifth century, awards were given to actors for their talents, thus turning acting into a distinct profession.

Social Position

In ancient Greece, the status of the actor was elevated over time. In the fifth century B.C., acting became a profession and as such was viewed with great admiration and respect. Roman actors, however, had a much more contemptible social status. Playwriting was not a sought-after trade; rather, it was bestowed upon one by heredity. Actors were often slaves or foreign captives who were made to perform in exchange for their freedom. Many Roman rulers passed laws forbidding certain high-ranking officials from entering theatres or consorting with those who participated in the theatre. Women rarely appeared in Roman productions and those who did so were limited to roles as mimes.

Origins of Roman Theatre

Roman theatre can easily be traced to Greek roots, as the Romans borrowed much of their theatre from Greek poets, even using Greek actors in Roman productions. It is believed that Rome had no intrinsic growth of poetry; rather, it was transplanted into Roman culture during a time when the Roman population sought to cultivate exotic luxuries. Livius Andronicus is credited with being the first Roman to imitate the theatre of the Greeks and is therefore credited with bringing theatre to Rome. The forms that were most easily converted from Greek to Roman were that of New Comedy and tragedy. Prior to Andronicus, the earliest spoken Roman productions were those of the Italian-import known as the Atellan Fables. The Greek form of theatre, in its transfer to Roman culture, was altered to better suit its Roman audience. The chorus, which historically sat in the orchestra area of the theatre, was removed, leaving the orchestra occupied by high-ranking spectators. Comedies were more easily received in Roman theatre than were tragedies.

Experience of Attending a Roman Play

Roman theatre usually consisted of a daytime production that lasted for approximately two hours, plays being most often performed immediately before or after the noon meal. Comedy was the dominant form of Roman theatre, using masks, wigs, costumes and makeup. Women were forbidden from participation in these plays, leaving the role of any female characters to be played by young boys. The earliest Roman venues consisted of very basic amphitheatres where the audience reclined on the ground and actors had very few resources at their disposal. As theatre evolved, the Roman stage was composed of a common street with several houses in the background and audiences were entertained by flute players during scene changes. Pompey the Great built the first Roman theatre auditorium in the year 55 B.C., where audiences were most entertained by outrageous and crude spectacles.

Roman Playwrights

Titus Maccius Plautus and Publius Terenius Afer

Both Plautus and Afer wrote comic plays. Their work, in fact, is the only surviving comic drama of the ancient Roman theatre. Plautus' work was very popular in his lifetime. His most notable works include Pot of Gold, The Menaechmi and Braggart Warrior. Like all Roman theatre, Plautus' comedy was based on the Greek New Comedies. He added allusions familiar to Roman culture as well as Latin dialog and poetic meters. Afer, who was better known as "Terence," was a freed Roman slave. The six plays he wrote that survive today are Andria, Hecyra, Heautontimoroumenos, Eunuchus, Phormio, and Adelphi. His plays used more complex plots, intriguing characters and even double-plots. The language used by Terence was more elegant than that of Plautus' plays, though Terence did not achieve the same popularity that Plautus did.

Roman Tragedy

Romans favored comedy above tragedy as a form of theatre, thus few tragic works have been preserved. The writings of Seneca provide the most notable remnants of the Roman tragedy. Additionally, Marcus Pacuvius and Lucius Accius are both noted for their imitations of Greek tragedy. The failure of the evolution of tragedy as a theatrical form in the hands of the Romans is in part due to their inability to reconcile the elements of song, dance and dialogue. The Romans seemed only able to successfully produce either a song and dance or a dialogue. The song and dance form evolved into a comedy that later lent itself to the pantomimus, or modern-day mime. Dialogue was used to enact tragic productions, usually involving one actor reciting tales to a small audience.

Decline of Roman Drama

The Roman theatre offered little entertainment for citizens, as their daily lives were already filled with shocking drama. It was common for Romans to see crucifixions, chained slaves paraded through streets and men killed by beasts in arena shows. The Roman culture had little tolerance socially or politically for the offerings of the theatre. They were more concerned with the matters of law than with the matters of the heart. The theatre productions borrowed from the Greeks were of a light-hearted and witty nature, lost on the Roman population, most of whom were unable to comprehend what they considered such trifles. The Roman Empire continued its expansion, requiring that the ruling class be distributed among newly acquired territories, which led to an overall decrease in the number of upper-class citizens in Rome. The remaining citizens, who were undereducated, were unable to understand the classical Latin language that was common in the theatre and were more intrigued by arena shows and circus performers than theatrics. The religious conversion of Roman emperor Constantine led to the outlaw of drama by Christian churches.

Indian Drama

Indian drama was born from an ancient tradition in which social and religious poetry was read at celebrations and feasts. According to Indian lore, theatre has mythical origins. The Indian culture believed there were three ages of man, each growing more distant from the will of the gods. According to this philosophy, humans began warring with each other, so the gods split the race into two sexes: men and women. The goal of the split was to create love; however, it only created desire for worldly things. Once the heart was drawn to outward desire, man lost his ability to be introspective. Pitying man's insatiable desires, the god Indra solicited the head god to create a spectacle so that humans could sate their appetite. The head god came up with the idea of Natya Veda or the Veda of the Theatre. Drama is the fifth Veda, a combination of the four earlier Vedas, which are dance, song, mimicry and passion.

India's Indigenous Drama

India's drama is unique in that its development was unaffected by foreign influence. Early European scholars held the view that Indian drama was originally an imitation of Greek drama but modern scholars know this to be untrue. The father of Indian drama, Bhrata, wrote many plays, thirteen of which exist today. The earliest one is dated 400 A.D. Indian plays had a unique structure in which they opened with a prayer followed by a narration of what was to come in the play. The narration would blend into the dialogue, giving way to the full performance. The majority of the plays' lines were in the form of prose in which beauty, morality and wisdom were described and reflected upon. Acts of violence and displays of affection were not part of Indian productions, though the plays did use stock characters such as the sneaky servant, the hero and the jester. Magic was the subject of many performances, having a character changed into an animal and requiring the intervention of the gods. The play would end with another prayer.

Medieval Plays

Minstrels traveled from town to town in medieval days offering some source of entertainment. The minstrel often dressed in a festive costume as he wandered between towns on the back of a mule. Minstrels, accompanied by their harps, would sing about the saints, heroes and scripture at gatherings and feasts. Enthusiasts would often award the minstrel with gifts and tokens and the most talented minstrels were hired for permanent service by ruling kings and bishops. Minstrels served an important role, paving the way for the reintroduction of drama in the Middle Ages after Greek drama had been outlawed by the Christian church. As the popularity of minstrels increased, Paris became the headquarters of minstrelsy, allowing the minstrels to band together into groups that could command rights and privileges exclusive to their craft.

Dramatic Literature in the Middle Ages

With the spread of Christianity, drama was outlawed as a vile and blasphemous spectacle. Rome experienced a fall from grace as the city of Constantinople became the new capital of civilization, during which time drama was mostly extinct. However, theatrics began to experience a rebirth after the human appetite for drama had lain dormant for years. Acrobats and traveling minstrels visited towns and performed for audiences and jesters and singers were called upon to entertain at the feasts of rulers. The dramatic plays written by famous Greek poets were looked upon as texts rather than scripts. People of the Middle Ages read the works of the ancient poets but did not feel the need to bring them to life in the form of theatrical production which the authors had intended. Dramatic literature of the Middle Ages existed primarily in the form of the ancient scripts with no new dramatic literature matching the form created by the ancient Greeks.

Rise of Drama

The drama of the Middle Ages had its origins in religion, born of the Christian church. Whereas the church had outlawed ancient theatre as blasphemous, the new forms of drama were created by the church as a means of spreading its beliefs. In order to best relay the dialogues that occurred in the stories relating to Jesus's life, priests would each read the lines spoken by one character in the story. Priests began acting out their lines to capture the interest of the congregation. These performances were common during Easter and the tradition soon extended to Christmas mass, where the Nativity story was retold through a theatrical production. The productions, however, began to grow into more elaborate and exaggerated tales that eventually bore little of the original intent. Priests could no longer exclusively handle the multitude of roles in a performance and were forced to invite laymen to participate. Eventually, the responsibility of these performances came to rest solely in the hands of laymen, who formed guilds and various organizations to handle each aspect of the productions.

English Cycles

The religious drama of the Middle Ages began as performances created by priests reenacting the stories of Jesus. The popularity of the productions grew to such an extent that the priests could no longer handle the various roles and the walls of the church could not accommodate the eager audiences. The productions were originally a unit portraying a certain episode in the life of Jesus or a saint. These units were eventually linked together to form a cohesive narrative called a Cycle. The Cycles could be broken into three main groups: Creation of man and the Old Testament, the Mystery of Atonement and the History of the Living Church. Old Testament plays tell of Adam and Eve in the garden, the corruption of mankind and the great flood. Atonement tells of the birth, life and sufferings of Jesus. The final Cycle tells of the lives of the saints, ministry of the apostles and of the Miracle of the Sacrament.

Origins of Interludes, Moralities and Farces

Interludes, moralities and farces were all forms of drama that made an appearance in the Middle Ages. During this time, the classical definitions of comedy and tragedy did not apply. All that was required for a production to be a tragedy was the staging of a fight. The morality play was a religious performance that used allegory, featuring characters named after certain qualities that could be seen in men: Greed, Pride, Avarice and Patience. Interludes and farces were the more secular performances of the Middle Ages. They featured a variety of performers including pantomimes, strolling players and professional actors. Many of the performers had the ability to act, sing, juggle, perform acrobatics and do magic. Farces were most noted for comic situations that used characters to which the audience could relate. Interludes were exactly what the name implies and were performed between acts of longer plays. Interludes, due to their brevity, were also commonly shown to entertain guests during celebrations and banquets.

Japanese Drama

Noh plays, created by Kwanami Kiotsugu, were the dominant form of drama in 14th-century Japan. Noh plays, featuring only male actors, incorporated the use of masks for the parts of women or gods. This form of theatre is characterized by its rigid structure and unchanging tradition. The play always began with a traveler who reveals his own name and the destinations to which he will travel in the play. A chorus describes the scenery and the thoughts of the traveler as he wanders the stage. Each place the traveler visits is inhabited by the Spirit of the Place, a ghost that must tell a story of suffering. The ancient legend of the site is revealed through a combination of dialogue among actors and recitations from the chorus. The play ends as the traveler prays for the ghost to find peace and then a song is sung to honor the gods.

Kabuki

Kabuki theatre began in Japan in the late 16th century. In the Japanese Edo Era, there was a strictly observed distinction between the warrior class and the common people. It was during this era that kabuki theatre began to grow in popularity. Kabuki theatre addresses the injustices of the people faced with the harsh laws of the feudal system. Kabuki served as a means of expression for the merchant class, whose wealth surpassed that of commoners, but whose status was not part of the warrior class. Kabuki began as a production in which the majority of players were female; however, due to concerns that the actresses were garnering undue attention, the government banned females from playing in kabuki performances in 1629. In kabuki theatre, female roles are played by males called onnagata. Kabuki is a unique form of theatre that combines several other types of Japanese theatre, taking inspiration from the Noh plays, puppet theatre (bunraku) and the realist productions of the 19th century.

Morality Plays

Near the beginning of the 15th century, the miracle plays of the Middle Ages gave way to plays of a different nature: morality plays. The miracle plays, started at the hands of priests, were reenactments of episodes in the life of Jesus. As these plays grew in popularity, priests and churches could no longer accommodate the various roles or the space needed for such large-scale productions. Left to the guilds, the miracle plays began to evolve into plays that focused not on the life of Jesus, but on the lives of everyday people. These plays used allegory to teach a moral lesson. Characters in morality plays had names such as Good Counsel, Pride and Avarice and the role of the Devil was popularized. While these plays strayed from using religious figures as characters, the message maintained a religious tone: good men were religious men.

Masques and Court Comedies

The theatre of the 16th century was divided into several groups, each suited to a particular class of people. Court Comedies were productions that were to be performed for the queen. Court Comedy was a variation on the popular pastoral drama form, many written by pastoral dramatist John Lyly. They were designed to sometimes subtly and other times overtly compliment Queen Elizabeth and the members of her court. Lyly's most notable work was the play Endimion, based upon the Greek myth of the shepherd named Endymion. Court Masques were introduced during the reign of Henry VIII in 1512. Players in masques were members of the king's court or even the royal family. Elaborate spectacles featuring music, costumes, scenery, mechanical effects and characters of mythological or allegorical origin, masques were limited to the private viewing by royalty as the performances were too costly to show in public theatres.

Origins of Elizabethan Theatre

The story of Robin Hood was popularized in Tudor England by the companies of roving players. Productions were held in barns and inns as public theatre was poorly regarded by English government of the time. The government even attempted to stop the strolling players from performing in 1572 with the passage of laws forbidding the practice. There was concern that the performances were apt to incite rebellion among the population and that the players were escorting diseases such as the plague from town to town. Only actors hired by noblemen were allowed to perform and from 1572 to 1574 only four noblemen obtained license to begin theatre companies. As in Roman theatre, women were forbidden from participation and female roles were played by young boys. The popularity of the performances grew to such an extent that James Burbage, in 1576, built a theatre in London to accommodate the large audiences.

William Shakespeare's Role

William Shakespeare is the most notable playwright of Elizabethan drama. Shakespeare's Henry VI was performed in 1592, followed by Hamlet, Romeo and Juliet, The Merchant of Venice, King Lear, Julius Caesar and Macbeth. Tudor audiences favored Shakespeare's plays involving the corrupt former kings of England and Elizabethan drama was both a source of entertainment and a podium for political propaganda. Shakespeare's work was well-received by the masses because it appealed to all classes and all levels of education. His work drew upon both current and classical theories of the organization of the universe and man's place within it. Shakespeare's work was greatly influenced by the events of his time but it also maintained a universality that can be appreciated even today. Christianity was no longer the singular source of religion; the authority of Rome was in question and capitalism was on the rise. The replacement of classic ideas with more modern knowledge and thought made audiences all the more receptive to the works of Shakespeare.

Regulations Imposed Upon Elizabethan Actors

In Elizabethan England, it was common for nobility to employ troupes of performers. These troupes began rapidly and some falsely claimed to be in the services of this or that lord. Members of false troupes were often beggars and vagabonds from whom nobility preferred to be distanced. In order to regulate the activity of false troupes, credentials were granted to credible performers and the aristocracy that maintained them. Elizabeth granted a royal patent, the first of its kind, to James Burbage and his four partners allowing them to perform anywhere in England. The only restriction was that political and religious subject matter could not be performed on stage, which led to objections by groups who had previously encouraged productions so long as they carried a religious message. In 1578 a total of six companies had a license to perform. In Elizabethan times, it was also the common practice for plays to be written by several authors with the actual owner being the company who performed the piece.

Impact of Reformation on German Drama

The Reformation was a catalyst of change all across Europe between 1517 and 1648. The movement began as an attempt to reform the Catholic church; however, it only managed to further divide the Christian sects. While the intentions of the Reformation were religious in nature, its ideas infiltrated all areas of society, including the theatre. Martin Luther, a German monk who later became a Protestant and a major supporter of Reformation, supported theatre and believed that certain books of the Bible had been written as plays. He viewed theatre as a means for spreading religious truth. Luther approved of Christmas plays depicting the birth of Jesus but he banned Passion plays, as he did not agree with the portrayal of Jesus's suffering. During this time, every part of the Bible became eligible for depiction through drama. Clown-plays also began during this time. The clown-play, or Sottie, featured a costumed actor who told jokes to lighten the often-somber mood of many plays. Sotties often occurred between acts of religious plays.

Origins of Drama in Spain

The Spanish culture was known for its ballads, which translate well into a dramatic performance. The ballads of Spain contained legends that were introduced to the area from various locations. Spain's battle with the Moors had ended, but the culture of the Moors had left an imprint upon the Spanish. Travelers from countries north of Spain brought tales of chivalry, knightly quests and heroic tournaments. These stories, along with oriental influences, all made their way into the already popular Spanish ballads. The ballads became more and more elaborate, requiring multiple singers and detailed costumes and scenery. The addition of these elements transformed the ballad into full-blown dramatic productions. The works of both Lope de Vega and Calderon de Barca characterize Spanish drama at its height.

Origins of Russian Drama

Drama made its way into Russia by way of Poland in the 12th century. The plays were known as Religious Dialogues or Histories. The performances were exclusive to monasteries until 1603 when they began to be performed in universities. The university performances were done in Polish or Latin, the earliest of which was a Latin piece entitled Adam, dated 1507, followed by a Polish piece entitled The Life of the Savior from His Entry into Jerusalem, which was dated 1533. While the origin of Russian drama is rooted in religious performances, Russia had a unique form of theatre called the Vertep. Vertep is a puppet theatre in which puppeteers control the dolls using strings attached to various parts of the doll. Vertep plays were used to depict religious stories. The word "Vertep" means "the secret place" and refers to the cave in which the Russian Orthodox Church believes Christ was born. Puppet characters include the Virgin Mary, Joseph, Jesus and various other figures central to the birth and life of Christ. Vertep plays eventually began to incorporate stories of a more secular nature.

Claque in French Theatres

The **claque** was an organized group of people hired to applaud during theatrical performances. The idea is believed to have originated when the emperor Nero required that five thousand soldiers chant his praise after a performance. Sixteenth-century poet, Jean Daurat, used this ancient practice as the foundation for the formation of the claque. "Claque" is derived from the French term "claquer," meaning to clap one's hands. Daurat's idea to ensure applause for performances was to give free tickets to any patrons who agreed to show their approval of the show. Eventually this practice became so popular that there developed a professional organization for claquers. In 1820 a man by the name of Sauton formed a business that supplied claquers to playwrights. It was the responsibility of the theatre manager to request the number of claquers necessary for a performance. The duties of the claquers reached beyond simple clapping. They could laugh at jokes, fake tears, encourage encores and generally ensure the audience remained happy.

Commedia Dell'arte

Commedia dell'arte, referring to improvisational drama, has its roots in Italy during the 16th and 17th centuries. These plays featured a scenario in which the characters were named and made aware of their relation to one another, the basic plot was outlined and the outcome was predetermined. The scenario, or canvas, was the skeleton of the play and it was up to the actors to provide the flesh. The subject of this theatre form seemed to focus on the intrigues of love and clever schemes. There were several stock character types, usually identified by masks, including a sneaky servant, a group of old men, a lady's maid, a doctor, a captain or adventurer, a jester and a hunchback. Each character had a stock of phrases and gestures to be used during a performance in the event that they could think of nothing original to fill in the blank spaces.

Creation of Opera

Opera, as a theatrical form, found its footing in 17th-century Italy. Musical science was a much sought-after field of study during this time in Italy. The Inquisition had limited the creative outlets in which previous artisans had found release. Music, however, remained one of the few forms of expression that the Inquisition allowed to exist. Poetry and literature began to decline and soon became secondary to the operatic form. Previous forms of drama, as they had been based on the Greek form, featured the dialogue of actors with a choral accompaniment in the background. In 1597 Italian poet Ottavio Rinuccini joined musicians Peri, Corsi and Caccini to create a piece in which this standard was reversed. The primary method of delivery became singing rather than dialogue and it became increasingly common for poets to write pieces specifically meant to be sung rather than spoken.

Review Video: Musicals vs Plays
Visit mometrix.com/academy and enter code: 537548

Bavarian Passion Play

In the year 1634, the citizens of the Bavarian city Ober-Ammergau began a ritual performance of a passion play depicting the life and death of Jesus. The year before, a disease swept through southern Bavaria killing many of the inhabitants, though the valley of Ammer remained free of the illness. Authorities would not let anyone into or out of the city for fear of contracting the deadly disease. However, a resident wishing to return to the Ammer valley after working in a neighboring town managed to secretly gain entrance into the city. He brought the deadly disease with him, leading to his own death and to the deaths of one fourth of the city's population. The remaining citizens made a pledge to God that if He protected them from being wiped out by the plague they would perform a Passion Play every ten years depicting the life and death of Jesus Christ. The town's legend states that from that moment the infected citizens were cured and the town remained free of the disease.

British Theatre

Attack by Puritans

Elizabethan drama became a popular attraction for many citizens, but its value soon came into question by Puritanical minds. Beginning in 1622, the popularity of theatre declined rapidly, and by 1642, laws demanded that theatres be closed. Lawmakers believed that theatre was an unfit indulgence for the times and that the minds of citizens should be focused upon the political strife occurring within the country. A 1647 law threatened to imprison and punish anyone who attempted to violate the no-theatre laws, followed by another law declaring all actors vagabonds and requiring the demolition of any theatre-related equipment and buildings. During this time, actors who were found in violation of the laws were fined, whipped, stripped of clothing and imprisoned. It was not until the Restoration that theatre regained its footing in England.

Comedy of Manners

Comedy of manners is a theatrical form credited to William Wycherley, George Etherege and William Congreve of 17th-century England, though Oscar Wilde rejuvenated the form in the 1890s. The comedy of manners is characterized by the distance between a society's selfish individual motives and simultaneous concern of projecting the image of being polite, well-mannered, educated citizens. This form of comedy became what is now known as Restoration Comedy. The style is characterized by its mocking of society and social norms and often targets marriage and love as the subjects of its mockery.

Restoration Theatre

Restoration theatre is also known as the comedy of manners. For almost twenty years prior to the return of the Stuart dynasty in England, theatre was outlawed. Charles II, ruling king of England in 1660, greatly influenced by his earlier years in Paris, allowed two companies of players to begin performing while he ruled England. William Davenant was in charge of the Duke's Company while Thomas Killigrew ran the King's Company. During this time, women began to appear on stage for the first time. The most notable playwrights of Restoration comedy include William Wycherly, George Etherege and William Congreve. Popular themes of Restoration comedy included the comical nature of love and marriage.

Origins of Pantomime

The **pantomime** maintained a very indistinctive role in productions until English actor Joseph Grimaldi reinvented the pantomime clown role in Harlequin. Clowns, especially pantomimes, were a common character in many forms of theatre, and were generally portrayed as the servant of a more important character. Grimaldi had a talent for visual tricks and general buffoonery and brought clowns to life through his elaborate mechanical tricks. Actor John Rich, in 1717, played the role of Harlequin in the pantomime Harlequin Executed. Harlequin was originally a speaking part, but people like John Rich only used gesture, movement and facial expression to convey the same sentiments that had previously been expressed only through words.

ORIGINS OF AMERICAN THEATRE

American theatre is believed to have originated early in the 18th century. The state of Virginia is recognized as the place in which American theatre first originated based on the 1716 construction of a theatre in Williamsburg. The New England provinces housed some of the earliest public theatres on record, despite their reputation for abhorrence of the theatre. The North as a whole seemed to view theatrical performances with much more contempt than their neighbors to the South. Few records exist relating to early American plays as a result of the multitude of laws passed prohibiting the performance or advertisement of such productions. Even with laws forbidding theatre, records of theatrical performances indicate that plays existed as early as 1702 in America.

GEORGE FARQUHAR'S COMEDY THE RECRUITING OFFICER

The Recruiting Officer holds a place in American history as the earliest play presented in New York of which a record exists. The play took place at the New Theatre in New York on December 6, 1732. The New Theatre was in a building that was owned by the city's acting governor, Rip Van Dam. The cast was composed of a group of actors who are believed to have come to America from London for the purpose of acting. The play itself, written by Irish-born George Farquhar, was written in London at a time when the town's recruiting officers were busy signing citizens into the military. The play had an overall witty tone and the dialogue was often bordering on indecent and raunchy by modern standards.

ORIGINS OF VAUDEVILLE

The creator of **vaudeville**, Tony Pastor, was a professional circus clown. Vaudeville is a type of variety show involving various types of acts, usually unrelated to each other. They included singers, dancers, acrobats, comedians, animal acts, impersonators and magicians. These shows were originally exclusive to bars and dance halls until Tony Pastor altered the style to make it suitable for the stage. In order to achieve the level of success that Pastor wanted, he knew that he had to make the shows appeal to highly reputed citizens. Pastor rejected the lewd acts that were typical of vaudeville shows and banned drinking and smoking in the theatre where the shows were held. Edward Albee II and B.F. Keith also played a large part in shaping the vaudeville theatre.

ORIGINS OF REALISM IN ITALIAN THEATRE

Realism made its debut in Italy following the fifty-year stint of Romanticism that began in 1852. Realism rejected the sentimental notion of the Romantics for a more practical view on life. Realists sought to examine the inner motives of the human being, desiring to use art as a means of depicting real life, as opposed to the Romantics, who used art to express what they wanted life to be like. Realists rejected the Romantic idea that life was rational and emotionally fulfilling. Realism was an attempt to objectively portray life through various forms of art. While this modern way of thinking was drawing organized opposition in France, Germany and England, Italy had no mass of opposition. Certain small groups and outspoken individuals criticized realism, but there was no organized movement to protest it in Italy as there was in other countries.

PROLETCULT

Proletcult was the term given to the Russian movement of 1917, which aimed to create a form of art that was devoid of bourgeois influence. The intent of Proletcult Theatre was to create productions in which political propaganda was not the sole content and purpose. The Proletcult Theatre served to remind Russia's working class that they were subservient to an arrogant and often tyrannous upper-class. This form of theatre was also called theatre of attractions because it did not use plot-driven scripts, but instead employed random dynamic spectacles to shock the audience or solicit some other form of emotion.

Theatre of the Absurd

Theatre of the Absurd, also called New Theatre and anti-theatre, is a phrase brought into existence by drama critic Martin Esslin. Esslin wrote a book bearing this title in 1962 addressing the type of play in which the human condition is decried as meaningless. The view of man's meaninglessness in the universe was a philosophy born of the Frenchman Albert Camus. Camus claimed that man had to resign himself to the fact that the universe defied logical explanation and could only be seen as absurd in its behavior. Esslin identified Eugene Ionesco, Samuel Beckett, Jean Genet, Arthur Adamov and Harold Pinter as the five defining playwrights of the absurdist movement. While this form of theatre was only recently assigned its own title, absurdist elements can be noticed in works as far back as those of Aristophanes. Absurdist elements can be identified in most plays predating the definition of Theatre of the Absurd, including Medieval morality plays and Elizabethan dramas. World War II, it is thought, readied the minds of playgoers for the themes presented in the Theatre of the Absurd.

Chinese Drama

Chinese drama is rooted in and still holds true to religious tradition, relying heavily on the principles, superstitions and symbols of Taoism, Confucianism and Buddhism. The use of various combinations of these religious beliefs allow for Chinese dramatists to create extravagant productions often set in unearthly realms. While both Buddhism and Taoism provide a rich supply of symbolism, Confucianism is a much more intangible belief that centers on the worship of ancestors. Confucianist belief is most often represented in the musical theatre of the Chinese and Buddhist beliefs are often seen represented in acts of buffoonery towards gods and demons. The involvement of Chinese religion in theatre can be simplified in the following way: Confucianism places emphasis on morality, humanity, and worship of ancestors; Buddhism involves the idea of suffering, the changing future, and worship of images; Taoism includes the idea of balance, evils in the present, and worship of spirits.

Symbolism

China is rich in national symbolism and this is reflected in its theatrical productions. Chinese drama views scenery as superfluous to a production, so it is implied through the words and actions of the actors. Lighting, also, is not an integral part of Chinese theatre. What the Chinese theatre lacks in scenery it makes up for in costumes, which are recreated accurately in the finest detail. The symbolism used in Chinese theatre is ancient and knowledge of its meaning has been handed down for generations, linking the past with the present. One such symbol is the yin-yang, which represents duality. Others are the dragon, a symbol of masculinity and heaven, and foxes, which symbolize deceit and trickery. Chinese drama also utilizes the sacred symbols known as the Hundred Antiques. These include the pearl, which prevents flood and fire; the coin, which signifies wealth; and jade, which brings justice. The Twelve Ornaments are also essential to Chinese theatre. These include images involving the sun, moon, dragon, birds and mountains.

History of Cleopatra

Since the time when the famous Queen of Egypt lived, her likeness has appeared in the dramatic productions of many artists. Samuel Daniel, in 1594, wrote a play entitled Cleopatra. In 1608, Elizabethan dramatist William Shakespeare wrote Antony and Cleopatra. John Fletcher and Francis Beaumont in their co-authored work, The False One, describe a Cleopatra much like the one found in Shakespeare's tale. In 1626, Thomas May wrote a play called The Tragedy of Cleopatra, Queen of Egypt. John Dryden's adaptation of Shakespeare's Antony and Cleopatra was entitled All for Love, featuring Cleopatra as a main character. American drama used Cleopatra as a central character in H.

Rider Haggard's 1890 drama, Cleopatra. In 1899, famed comic dramatist George Bernard Shaw wrote a five-act play entitled Caesar and Cleopatra.

Superstitions Involving Theatre

Theatrical participants ranging from managers to actors, even today, hold some of the same superstitions that originated in the early years of theatre. One such superstitious belief is that blue scenery robs actors of wealth or lead to death. Blue scenery, in early European theatre, was allowed only if silver ornaments were hung, as silver was believed to ward off evil. Another superstition warns that Sunday rehearsals ensure disaster for actors and patrons. This arose from the death of New York's Grand Opera House manager after he called for a Sunday rehearsal. Another belief is that on the opening night of a new play, the first person admitted cannot be the holder of a free ticket or the play will fail. The black cat is seen as a sign of good fortune in theatres, while peacock feathers are renowned as bad luck. The luck in carrying a rabbit's foot led early actor Edmund Kean to dig up the remains of a deceased actor and procure one of his toe bones, to which Kean later attributed his great success.

Evolution of Stage Lighting

In its earliest days, theatre lighting was limited to the effects that could be harnessed from the sun, moon and stars. Early theatre was presented during daylight hours and the light that was cast upon the stage was controlled by nature. It can be assumed that theatre stages may have been built with this in mind. It is possible the stages were built in such a way as to cast shadows in the necessary places while positioning the most intense rays of light in others. Italian theatre began making use of candles for lighting effects in the 16th century: English theatre, in the 17th century. Oil lamps, in the 18th century, became the lighting method of choice. Gas lighting became available in the 19th century and the first theatre to use it was the Chestnut Street Theatre in Philadelphia. The first theatre to utilize electricity, discovered in 1879, was London's Savoy Theatre. In America, Boston's Bijou Theatre was the first to install electric lighting.

Time Line of Illumination Techniques

Specific illumination, which became the preferred lighting method in the mid-19th century, involves a controlled shaft of light that can focus and highlight any part of the stage. The first form of specific illumination was the limelight, also called a calcium light, and was invented by Thomas Drummond. Arc lamps, powered by a battery, did not become a practical source of lighting until the invention of the generator. The invention of the incandescent spotlight soon replaced the arc light in theatres. The baby lens, invented by Louis Hartmann, was followed by Thomas Edison's invention of a concentrated filament for use in a spotlight. By the 1920s, spotlights were the predominant form of lighting.

Lighting Designers

Adolphe Appia

The writing of Adolphe Appia is said to have given rise to modern lighting theory. Appia described three types of lighting in one of his plays: diffused light, creative light and painted light. He also identified four lighting cues: dazzling sunlight, the blood-red light of sunset, twilight and hazy darkness.

Norman Bel Geddes

Norman Bel Geddes, while best known for his impressive and large theatrical designs, also contributed to modern lighting techniques. Bel Geddes built a model theatre with an electric lighting system. He used this model to experiment with light sources and positions until he discovered the optimal combinations.

Robert Edmond Jones

Robert Edmond Jones, often referred to as the father of American scene design, used minimal scenery but dramatic lighting effects. One of his most memorable pieces was his staging of Macbeth. The entire performance took place on a bare stage with three giant moveable witch masks gazing down upon the performance. Jones used only single spotlights to isolate the acting areas.

Abe Feder

Abe Feder, who studied at what is now Carnegie-Mellon University, was the first to coin the title "lighting designer." During his career, Feder was the lighting designer for over 300 Broadway shows. Feder was also known for his architectural lighting design, having created the lighting for the Empire State building, the RCA/GE building in Rockefeller Center and the United Nations building.

Jean Rosenthal

Jean Rosenthal is best known for her lighting design in musicals from the 1950s and 1960s. She is credited as the inventor of dance lighting.

Peggy Clark

Peggy Clark was the first female to hold the position of president in the United Scenic Artist organization. She assisted in scene design and was the lighting designer for several Broadway plays.

Contributions of Lope de Vega

Lope de Vega was a Madrid-born dramatist whose work is viewed as some of the best drama to come out of 16th- and 17th -century Spain. De Vega's work was characterized by his desire to place emphasis upon the individual. It is believed that de Vega's works were so popular that dramatists such as Voltaire, Shakespeare, Moliere and Marlowe all borrowed from de Vega's vast selection of writings. Lope de Vega's work consisted of four distinct styles: chivalrous drama, historical heroic drama, social life drama and sacred plays. It is believed that de Vega wrote near 2,200 plays in his lifetime, of which 481 exist today. Lope de Vega created Spanish drama from the Spanish tradition, folklore and stories that were native to his country. He ignored the classical traditions of the ancient Greeks and created some of the first plays belonging to the genre of romantic drama.

Contributions of Calderon de la Barca

Calderon de la Barca is best known for his ability to write both comic and tragic dramas. De la Barca, though he could write comedy, was most skilled with tragic drama. Much like Lope de Vega, de la Barca ignored the classical tradition of writing and instead drew material from the stories and culture of his native land. Of the hundreds of plays that have been credited to de la Barca only 181 have been proven authentic. His work often featured supernatural themes, grim humor and innovative plots. Much of de la Barca's work was influenced by his devout Catholicism just as much of his work was limited by his refusal to accept modern thinking. He was deeply medieval in his beliefs and resisted modern ideas, yet he still managed to produce some of the best romantic dramas of 17th-century Spain.

Jean Baptiste Poquelin de Moliere

In many circles Moliere, whose birth name was Jean Baptiste Poquelin, is considered one of the greatest comic dramatists of all time. The name Moliere was taken by the young Poquelin as a stage name but it soon became so popular that his original surname effectively ceased to exist. He was known for both writing and acting in many French satires that still exist today. Moliere's play titled Tartuffe is considered one of his most successful works. Tartuffe was first performed for Louis XIV but was attacked by 17th century censors, who managed to suppress the play for three years after its debut. Moliere trained in France and traveled with a company of actors for over twelve years developing his craft. Among his most notable works are Don Juan, The Misanthrope and The Learned Ladies. Moliere died during a stage performance after a coughing fit caused a blood vessel to burst.

Contributions of Voltaire

Francois-Marie Arouet was a famed French playwright during the Enlightenment. He was more commonly known by the name Voltaire, which he assumed following his first successful production in 1718. Voltaire, classically educated by Jesuit priests, was known for his rebellion against intolerance, which landed him in jail on multiple occasions. Voltaire was exiled from France for his radical views at the time and he sought refuge in England. He traveled to several places, including Brussels and Holland. One of Voltaire's earliest works, written when he was only 19, is Oedipe. The success of this play was followed by Brutus, Zaire and Eriphile. Voltaire is best noted for his use of exotic influence in his works. He used plot material from foreign lands including China and South America. Voltaire's works extended to works of poetry, prose and letter writing.

William Hallam

William Hallam was a theatre actor-manager hailing from London. Hallam, recognizing America as rife with possibility for theatre arts, decided to create a company of players that he could send there. Hallam charged Robert Upton with traveling to America and preparing theatres for his vision; however, Upton took the money Hallam gave him and joined another company of players in America, completely neglecting the mission for which he was sent. Despite losing the aid of Robert Upton, Hallam decided to continue as planned. William Hallam, while not the first to introduce drama to America, did much for establishing its permanence. He put together a company of players who had the talent to execute a variety of theatrical genres, thus allowing the company to offer a multitude of productions.

Lewis Hallam

Lewis Hallam came to America in 1753 with the acting company sent over by his brother William Hallam. Lewis and his wife were both members of this theatre company, which presented a signed testament of the members' ability and character from Governor Dinwiddie, the British advocate for colonial expansion in America. Despite the support of Dinwiddie, colonial magistrates refused to issue a license to Lewis Hallam for theatrical performances in New York. Hallam rousted public interest through petitions and was soon granted license to perform. He produced twenty-one plays during a six-month stay in New York, including comedies, tragedies and farces. Once the company had solidified itself in New York, the members decided to pursue similar fame in Philadelphia. Hallam faced the same reluctance from authorities in Philadelphia but soon managed to overcome them. Hallam remained in Philadelphia for two months before the company retired to the West Indies. It is here that Lewis Hallam passed away after a long illness. Hallam is credited as part of the original company that solidified the place of American theatre.

George II, Duke of Saxe-Meiningen

The Duke of Saxe-Meiningen has been dubbed the first modern director. His works influenced theatrical pioneers including actor/manager Andre Antoine Konstantin Stanislavski. George II was known for designing his own sets, training his actors and conducting every rehearsal. The Duke paid special attention to details and planned each moment of each scene. He preferred to have stage props such as chairs, chimneys and doors that were real rather than drawn or created. The Duke created his own design rules, exemplified by his utilization of steps and levels to divide the stage into separate areas. . He refused to set anything in the middle of the stage, believing that a pleasing visual composition was one in which the middle of the picture was not centered on the middle of the stage. He also used various natural materials such as tree branches to hide technical equipment above the stage. In order to craft the most effective production, the Duke felt it was necessary to observe all movements on stage from visual and acoustic perspectives of various audience positions.

Henrik Ibsen

Norwegian native Henrik Ibsen is best known for bringing the French play to its height of perfection. Ibsen was not only a modern dramatist, but also a theatre manager and philosopher. Henrik Ibsen's work was prone to reflect his changing ideals. One work would proclaim the value of an ideal while in another work he would decry the selfsame value as worthless. He addressed this difference of opinion in his work titled An Enemy of the People, stating that most truths are obsolete after twenty years. His work further exposed what he saw as the social prejudices of his time. He extolled upon the value of the individual and each person's right to choose their own path in life. Ibsen believed that the true destiny of each man and the ultimate source of happiness was being true to one's self. Ibsen's ideas were not well-received during his lifetime and he was attacked by other playwrights for his seemingly ridiculous ideas.

Lewis Carroll

Lewis Carroll is the pen name of Charles Lutwidge Dodgson, author of "Alice's Adventures in Wonderland" (1865), and its sequel "Through The Looking Glass" (1871). His literary reputation rests on these two children's books, although he wrote several other novels including "The Hunting of the Shark" (1876), "A Tangled Tale" (1885), and "Sylvie and Bruno" (1889). Carroll also wrote several significant works on logic and mathematics. "Alice" was inspired by his favorite child-friend, Alice Liddell, and her two sisters to whom he related the story. Carroll was born in England in 1832 and became a mathematics teacher and resident Scholar of Christ Church College, Oxford. He assumed his pen name to protect his academic reputation that might be affected by authoring children's books. "Alice" brought him instant celebrity and served as an entreé to Victorian society. Carroll remained at Oxford until his death in 1898.

Louisa May Alcott

Louisa May Alcott is one of America's beloved children's writer, novelist, and short-story writer. Alcott began her publishing career writing popular "dime novels" under pseudonyms to make a living. The publication of "Little Women" in 1868, and its huge popularity, allowed her to pursue serious fiction thereafter. "Little Women" is a fond narrative of family life based partially on her own family. It is a romantic, yet realistic novel with strong and memorable characters. Alcott's later novels include "Little Men" (1871) and "Rose in Bloom" (1876), both written for young readers. Her best adult fiction includes "Moods" (1864), a novel of married life, and "Work" (1874), a story based on her financial problems. Alcott was born in Boston in 1832 and reared in nearby Concord. Her father was the famous Transcendentalist thinker, Bronson Alcott. She died in 1888.

Mark Twain

Mark Twain, the pen name of Samuel Langhorne Clemens, was a true American voice in literature. Humorist, novelist, and travel writer, he is best known for "Tom Sawyer" (1876), and "The Adventures of Huckleberry Finn" (1884), beloved novels with memorable characters and undertones of social concern. "Life on the Mississippi " (1883) was an autobiographical account of his days on a riverboat. Twain's acid humor, and stories of a fading rural America, made him one of the most popular figures of his day. Born in 1835 in Hannibal, Missouri, Twain who was self-educated, became a journalist and sometimes printer. His literary success made him a popular lecturer in America and Europe. His travels abroad provided Twain with the material for the satirical "A Connecticut Yankee in King Arthur's Court " (1889), and "The Innocents Abroad"

(1869). His later life was marred by tragedy including the death of his wife and two daughters, as well as financial difficulty. He died in America in 1910.

Thomas Hardy

Hardy was an English novelist, playwright, and short-story writer. His dark works, often drawn from his own experience, include his first novel "Far from the Maddening Crowd" (1874), a tale of a strong woman and her three lovers. Hardy followed this modest success with four powerful novels, "Jude the Obscure" (1895), "The Return of the Native" (1878), "Tess of the D'Urbervilles" (1891), and "The Mayor of Casterbridge" (1896). All these volumes showcased Hardy's skills as storyteller and creator of strong characters. Hardy's poetry is also considered to be some of the best of his time. Hardy was born in Dorchester in Southwest England in 1840. Hardy was trained as an architect, which he gave up for writing when he achieved success. With death of his wife, Hardy was guilt ridden and his grief fueled the writing of his greatest poetry, "Poems of 1912-13". Hardy married again and lived until 1928.

Contributions of Richard D'Oyly Carte

Richard D'Oyly Carte is recognized as the manager of the Royalty Theatre in London, as well as the creator of English comic-opera. D'Oyly booked a short opera to be performed at the Royalty Theatre. In order to make the event longer in length, he hired W.S. Gilbert and Arthur Sullivan to write a one-act comic opera, which they entitled Trial by Jury. The performance was a huge success and D'Oyly booked many of Gilbert and Sullivan's productions in the various theatres he managed. Examples of comic-operas include The Sorcerer, Patience and The Pirates of Penzance. Carte also owned and directed multiple theatre companies in both England and America. Among the many theatre houses he owned in London were the Opera Comique, the Savoy Theatre, and the English Opera House, later to become the Palace Theatre. D'Oyly Carte was also a musical composer, creating such works as Dr. Ambrosius: His Secret and Marie.

Robert Louis Stevenson

Robert Louis Stevenson was a Scottish essayist, novelist, poet, and short-story writer. After writing for weeklies for a few years, his "Treasure Island" (1883) brought him acclaim and wealth. Stevenson followed this success with "Kidnapped" (1886), "The Strange Case of Dr. Jekyll and Mr. Hyde" (1886), and "The Master of Ballantrae" (1889), all critical and financial successes. Stevenson also wrote a book of verse for children, "A Child's Garden of Verses"(1885). His swashbuckling tales and colorful language engaged the fancy of the public, and he retired a wealthy man. Stevenson was born in Edinburgh in 1850 and was educated in law. His life was tainted by chronic tuberculosis, and he sought cures and more healthy climates all over the world. Stevenson finally found the relief he sought in Samoa, where he settled and lived the last years of his life. He died there in 1894, at the young age of 44.

David Belasco

American-born David Belasco was a playwright, director and producer who got his start in theatre in San Francisco, where he was born. He worked as script copier and callboy in various theatres until his playwright skills were noticed. He then moved to New York and became a stage manager for the Madison Square Theatre before becoming an independent producer in 1859. His most notable works are Madame Butterfly and The Girl of the Golden West. Belasco wrote, directed or produced most of the plays shown on Broadway between 1884 and 1930. He also furthered naturalism in the theatre by using unconventional methods, such as placing scents in air ducts in the theatre to heighten the reality of a scene. He used working washing machines and dryers in his productions and his actors would cook real food if the script called for scenes involving eating.

Belasco's attention to detail also gave rise to some advanced lighting techniques, which he used to create a mood or evoke a certain setting.

Contributions of George Bernard Shaw

Irish-born socialist George Bernard Shaw authored over sixty plays in his lifetime, most of which was comedy but it always contained some form of social or political propaganda. Shaw claimed that the primary reason of high-writing was to sway the masses to his way of thinking. Shaw was considered a freethinker of the 20th century. He spoke out for women's rights and demanded equality of income. When he was awarded the Nobel Prize in 1925 for literature, he accepted the award but refused the money associated with it. Shaw's work was greatly influenced by Norwegian playwright Henrik Ibsen. In addition to being a dramatist, Shaw was a literary critic and an accomplished public speaker, especially as a spokesman for socialism.

Sir Arthur Conan Doyle

Conan Doyle's contribution to literature was the enigmatic detective, Sherlock Holmes. Conan Doyle based his character on a former professor at the University of Edinburgh. Holmes first appeared in 1887 in " A Study in Scarlet", and more stories of the master of deductive reasoning appeared in magazines of the day. These stories were collected and published as "The Adventures of Sherlock Holmes" in 1892. Most memorable among the Holmes novels include "The Hound of the Baskervilles" (1902), " The Valley of Fear" (1915), and "The Sign of Four" (1890). Holmes also wrote a number of popular historical romances. Conan Doyle was born in London in 1859 and educated at Edinburgh. He trained as a physician and practiced medicine in Southsea from 1882-90. The success of his writing allowed him to largely retire from medicine.

Adolphe Appia

Adolphe Appia shaped modern day stagecraft through his early theories involving staging, lighting and the use of space. He believed that space was a dynamic element that could be utilized to convey a much more realistic feel for audiences. Appia began studying opera and soon decided that it did not offer the fluidity and staging that properly accentuated the human presence. He theorized that stage space would be better incorporated into a performance if it contained steps, ramps, platforms and drapes, all of which could be unified with actors through the use of lighting. Appia studied various operatic scenes in differing light and staging scenarios in order to find the best combinations. He published books on his theories, most notable of which are The Staging of Wagner's Musical Dramas, Music and Stage Setting and The Work of Living Art.

Contributions of Konstantin Stanislavsky

Russian-born Konstantin Stanislavsky is one of the most influential figures of the 20th century with regard to the acting process. He began acting at the age of 14 and as he got older moved to producing and directing. Stanislavsky's approach to acting was created over a forty-year period. He invented a method called the Stanislavsky System, which was at the forefront of modern psychological and emotional aspects of acting. His system became known as the Method. The fundamental principle of the Method is that it is the actor's primary responsibility to be believed. Method acting uses emotional memory. This approach was a novel idea in the acting world because it required actors to use parts of their own life, memories and personality while acting, whereas previous methods required actors to be blank slates, always ready to assume a new character's identity.

Contributions of Gordon Craig

Gordon Craig is credited with being one of the most influential faces of modern theatre. Craig's ideas on theatre can be seen in his 1904 book The Art of the Theatre. While many of Craig's peers believed that stage-directors should be merely interpreters, Craig saw the stage-director as a creator. It is a commonly held notion that the dramatist, director and actor align in a hierarchal form in which the actor is told what to do by the director, who is interpreting the words written by the dramatist. Craig believed that the role of the director superseded that of both the actor and the dramatist. He believed that theatre needed to be unified under the guidance of the director. One of Craig's most controversial philosophies is that theatre can function independently of literature. He felt that impulses of the director or even the actor were sufficient to create a performance and that a script was not essential.

Vsevolod Emilevich Meyerhold

Russian-born Vsevolod Emilevich Meyerhold performed the roles of actor, director and producer during his lifetime and was known for his socialist tendencies. He studied law for a short time, but soon abandoned law school for the Moscow Philharmonic Dramatic School, which was co-founded by Konstantin Stanislavski. Meyerhold went on to act in and direct several productions, each of which served as an opportunity for him to experiment with staging methods. He incorporated symbolism into most of his work because he believed it was a crucial part of any dramatic production. Stanislavski despised Meyerhold's work and wanted nothing to do with his work. One of Meyerhold's goals was to reinvent Commedia dell'arte in a more contemporary style. Meyerhold's acting technique was in direct opposition to Stanislavski's method. Meyerhold believed that emotion could be conveyed through use of practiced postures and gestures regardless of the actor's actual emotional state.

Freie Bühne

Freie Bühne is a German phrase meaning free theatre. The Freie Bühne was a German society in Berlin that sponsored performances that were banned or censored by commercial theatres. The origins of the society coincide with the visitation of Paris' Théâtre Libre to Berlin. Otto Brahm, theatre critic and proponent of naturalism, was part of the group that formed to create the society. One of the first works the society sponsored was Henrik Ibsen's Ghosts. Vor Sonnenaufgang, written by Gerhart Hauptmann, was the second play performed. This production was the first naturalistic play to be performed in Germany, relating a tale of a family's downfall at the hands of alcoholism, corruption and desire for wealth. The society ceased to exist in 1893 after only four years.

Antonin Artaud

Antonin Artaud was a French poet, playwright, actor and director. Artaud aspired to create a form of theatre where actors would serve as an extension of the audience's most repressed realities. Artaud, who was a follower of the surreal movement, unfortunately suffered from mental problems and was hospitalized repeatedly throughout his lifetime. Most noted for his concept of the theatre of cruelty described in his book, Theatre and its Double, he believed that theatre needed to awaken people to the truths that they struggled to suppress in their daily lives. He rejected the idea that theatre could only exist as a story involving a character who, when faced with a problem, could find resolution by the end of the play. The cruelty Artaud spoke of was not physical violence but a mental deliverance in which actors were presented as characters stripped of preconceived notions and outward appearances, the ultimate goal being to force audiences to see reality for what it was and not what others would have them believe it to be.

Eugène Ionesco

Romanian-native Eugene Ionesco is credited with creating the theatre of the absurd. Ionesco was born in 1909, but his family relocated to Paris, where he remained for sixteen years. In 1925, Ionesco returned to Romania with his father after his parents divorced. After a period of study,

Ionesco wrote his first play in 1948. Ionesco's work rejected logical plots and standard character development. His plays were a comic portrayal of what he viewed as the absurdity of reality: man's existence as devoid of meaning in a universe ruled only by chance. Ionesco was attacked by critics for the lack of realism in his work and his rebuttal to these criticisms was that his writing was an effort to revitalize language and communication by saying things in a new way. People were shocked by Ionesco's views of drama and they either loved or hated it. In either case, talk of his work brought it increasing recognition. In 1962 Ionesco's niche in theatre history was defined by theatre critic Martin Esslin, who coined the term "theatre of the absurd" to describe Ionesco's work.

Contributions of Gao Xingjian

Chinese-born dramatist Gao Xingjian was educated in the People's Republic with a love of theatre nurtured by his actress mother. His love of theatre and freethinking resulted in his incarceration in a re-education camp for six years. Under threat of persecution from Communist leader Mao Zedong, Gao Xingjian wrote in secrecy, believing that literature was a link to human consciousness. His works were not published until 1980 and in 1981 his plays were performed at the Beijing People's Art Theatre. His plays were influenced by Samuel Beckett, Antonin Artaud and Bertolt Brecht, causing his work to be dubbed the "Chinese Theatre of the Absurd." Xingjian's play Bus Stop was based on Beckett's Waiting for Godot. Bus Stop was viewed as highly controversial and received much scrutiny from Communist Party authorities. Though the Chinese government could not accept the value of his work, Xingjian was awarded the Nobel Prize in Literature in 2000.

Major Contributors

- **Alfred Bunn** was an English theatrical manager who managed London's Drury Lane Theatre, Birmingham's Theatre Royal and London's Convent Garden. He also attempted to establish the opera in England.
- **James Burbage**, an English actor, erected the first theatre in London called The Theatre in Shorditch and started the Blackfriar's Theatre.
- **Christopher Marlowe** was famed for his blank verse. Marlow's plays include Tamburlaine, Doctor Faustus and The Jew of Malta He was an Elizabethan dramatist who preceded Shakespeare, a poet and a fictional writer.
- **William Congreve**, an English dramatist, was famed for his comic dramas.
- **Gao Xingjian** created what is known as the Chinese Theatre of the Absurd. Xingjian won a Nobel Prize for Literature in 2000.
- **John Heywood**, English dramatist, transformed morality plays from the Middle Ages into modern productions by changing the allegorical characters into real people.
- **John Lyly** brought the pastoral to England and created the form of Court Comedy.
- **Ben Johnson**, a London-born dramatist, was famed for works of comedy and satire.
- **Hans Sachs** was a German shoemaker, writer, singer and songwriter. He wrote over 208 plays during the 16th century.
- **Lope de Rueda** was a Spanish actor, manager and playwright who invented the Spanish version of the short farce called pasos.
- **Emile Zola** was a French writer who supported naturalism.
- **Honore de Balzac** was a French writer who is credited as the founding father of realism in European literature.
- **Henry Becque** was a 19th-centuryFrench playwright who incorporated both naturalism and realism into his work.
- **Aphra Behn** was the first female English playwright and a British spy.

MAJOR PLAYWRIGHTS

- **Ionesco**: Rhinoceros, The Chairs, The Bald Soprano, The Lesson, The Killer, Exit the King, Hunger and Thirst and A Stroll in the Air.
- **Shaw**: Pygmalion, Caesar and Cleopatra, Androcles and the Lion, The Doctor's Dilemma, Candida and Major Barbara.
- **Marlowe**: Tamburlaine, Doctor Faustus, The Jew of Malta, Edward II and The Massacre at Paris.
- **Congreve**: The Way of the World, The Old Bachelor, Love for Love, The Double-Dealer and The Mourning Bride.
- **Xingjian**: Absolute Signal, Wilderness Man, Between Life and Death and Dialogue.
- **De Vega**: The Star of Seville, The Sheep Well, The Foolish Lady and Punishment Without Revenge.
- **De la Barca**: Devotion of the Cross, Life is a Dream and The World is a Fair.
- **Ben Johnson**: The Alchemist, Every Man out of His Humor, The Sad Shepherd, The Masque of Blackness.
- **Hans Sachs**: Lucretia, Virginia.
- **Lope de Rueda**: Eufemia, Medora, Armelina.
- **Giovanni Verga**: The She-Wolf, In the Porter's Lodge, The Wolf Hunt, The Fox Hunt, and Rustic Chivalry.
- **J. M. Barrie**: Peter Pan, Mary Rose, What Every Woman Knows, Quality Street, The Admirable Crichton.
- **Pierre Beaumarchais**: The Barber of Seville, The Marriage of Figaro.
- **Samuel Beckett**: Waiting for Godot, Endgame, and Happy Days.
- **Bertolt Brecht**: Baal, A Man's a Man, The Threepenny Opera, The Life of Galileo, Mother Courage, The Caucasian Chalk Circle, The Visions of Simone Machard.
- **Anton Chekhov**: The Seagull, Uncle Vanya, The Cherry Orchard, and The Three Sisters.
- **George Cohan**: Seven Keys to Baldplate, The Little Millionaire, Little Nelly Kelly, and Forty-five Minutes from Broadway.
- **Richard Brinsley Sheridan**: The Rivals, The Critic, A Trip to Scarborough, and The School for Scandal.
- **Friedrich von Schiller**: The Robbers, Don Carlos, Maria Stuart.
- **Johann Wolfgang von Goethe**: Faust, The Lover's Caprice, Clavigo, Egmont, Stella, Iphigenia in Tauris, Torquato Tasso.

Chapter Quiz

Ready to see how well you retained what you just read? Scan the QR code to go directly to the chapter quiz interface for this study guide. If you're using a computer, simply visit the online resources page at **mometrix.com/resources719/nystcetheater166** and click the Chapter Quizzes link.

Responding to and Analyzing Theater

Critical Response to Drama

Reading Drama

Despite the inherent problems in reading drama, there are strategies that are useful in developing skills and techniques to enrich the experience.

1. Read the play through initially at one sitting, then reread it making notes on dominant themes, characters, and difficult passages. Reading without pausing helps give the material a flow that can be missing from drama text. This also helps clarify the major themes and broad outlines of the work.
2. As plays are written to be spoken aloud, it is a good practice to read them aloud to better capture the verbal cadences and linguistic features not evident in written text. Reading aloud can sometimes give a better sense of a passage and help understand difficult text by placing it into context. The language of drama is keyed to oral production and replicating this is an excellent tool.
3. Reading in a group is a way to catch the flavor of characters interacting in a drama. One can find a better a sense of how the dialogue functions and therefore the roles of various characters in the play are more easily understood.

Reading Dramatic Dialogue

Dramatic dialogue can be difficult to interpret and changes depending upon the tone used and which words are emphasized. Where the stresses, or meters, of dramatic dialogue fall can determine meaning. Variations in emphasis are only one factor in the manipulability of dramatic speech. Tone is of equal or greater importance and expresses a range of possible emotions and feelings that cannot be readily discerned from the script of a play. The reader must add tone to the words to understand the full meaning of a passage. Recognizing tone is a cumulative process as the reader begins to understand the characters and situations in the play. Other elements that influence the interpretation of dialogue include the setting, possible reactions of the characters to the speech, and possible gestures or facial expressions of the actor. There are no firm rules to guide the interpretation of dramatic speech. An open and flexible attitude are essential in interpreting dramatic dialogue.

Reading Dramatic Action

Stage directions: Action is a crucial element in the production of a dramatic work. Many dramas contain little dialogue and much action. In these cases, it is essential for the reader to carefully study stage directions and visualize the action on the stage. Benefits of understanding stage directions include knowing which characters are on the stage at all times, who is speaking to whom, and following these patterns through changes of scene. Stage directions also provide additional information, some of which is not available to a live audience. The nature of the physical space where the action occurs is vital, and stage directions help with this. The historical context of the period is important in understanding what the playwright was working with in terms of theaters and physical space. The type of staging possible for the author is a good guide to the spatial elements of a production.

ADVANTAGES OF READING DRAMA AS TEXT

An oft-heard criticism of reading drama is that the experience pales when compared to watching a performance. There are however some advantages to reading drama as text:

1. Freedom of point of view, and perspective that the written text does not. Text is free of interpretations of actors, directors, producers, and technical staging.
2. Additional information - the text of a drama may be accompanied by notes or prefaces placing the work in a social or historical context. Stage directions may also provide relevant information about the author's purpose. None of this is typically available at live or filmed performances.
3. Study and understanding - difficult or obscure passages may be studied at leisure and supplemented by explanatory works. This is particularly true of older plays with unfamiliar language which cannot be fully understood without an opportunity to study the material.

USING YOUR IMAGINATION

A play is written to be spoken aloud. The drama is in many ways inseparable from performance. Reading drama ideally involves using imagination to visualize and recreate the play with characters and settings. The reader stages the play in his imagination, watching characters interact and developments unfold. Sometimes this involves simulating a theatrical presentation, while some may imagine the events happening before them. In either case, the reader is imagining the unwritten in order to recreate the dramatic experience. Novels present some of the same problems, but a narrator will provide much more information about the setting, characters, inner dialogues and many other supporting details. In drama, much of this is missing and we are required to use our powers of projection and imagination to taste the full flavor of the dramatic work. There are many empty spaces in reading dramatic texts that must be supplied by the reader to fully appreciate the work.

Relationship of Theatre to Other Art Forms and Other Disciplines

CHILDREN'S LITERATURE

Children's literature is designed to be read and enjoyed primarily by young readers. Early children's literature was written exclusively for educational purposes. Beginning in the middle of the 18th century, children's books were written to entertain as well as edify. Adventure stories for boys became popular in the 19th century, as did fiction designed for girls, such as Louisa May Alcott's "Little Women" (1868), and Johanna Spyri's " Heidi" (1880). Mark Twain and Robert Louis Stevenson became important writers of children's fiction during this time.

Recent years have emphasized more realism in children's literature. Opposed to the traditional view of shielding children from the realities of life, many now advocate books that are not only realistic but tragic, providing an opportunity for catharsis for young readers. An example of this type of fiction is William Armstrong's "Sounder" (1969), a novel of the evils of a segregated society written for young readers.

SOCIOLINGUISTICS

Sociolinguistics is the study of the relationship between language and the structure of society. It takes into account the social backgrounds of both the speaker and the addressee, the relationship between the speaker and the addressee, and the context and manner of the interaction. Because the emphasis in sociolinguistics is on language use, the analysis of language in this field is typically based on taped recordings of everyday interactions. The sociolinguists seek to discover universal properties of languages, attempting to analyze questions such as "do all languages change in the same ways"? Answers are sought to the larger questions about universals in society in which language plays a major role. The multifaceted nature of language and its broad impact on many areas of society make this field an exciting and cutting-edge part of linguistics.

AESTHETICS

Aesthetics is the study of sensory or sensori-emotional values, sometimes called judgments of sentiment and taste. Aesthetics is a subdiscipline of axiology, a branch of philosophy, and is closely associated with the philosophy of art. Aesthetics studies new ways of seeing and of perceiving the world. Judgments of aesthetic value clearly rely on our ability to discriminate at a sensory level. Aesthetics examines what makes something beautiful, sublime, disgusting, fun, cute, silly, entertaining, pretentious, discordant, harmonious, boring, humorous or tragic.

Aesthetic judgments usually go beyond sensory discrimination. For David Hume, delicacy of taste is not merely "the ability to detect all the ingredients in a composition," but also our sensitivity "to pains as well as pleasures, which escape the rest of mankind." Thus, the sensory discrimination is linked to a capacity for pleasure. For Immanuel Kant, "enjoyment" is the result when pleasure arises from sensation, but judging something to be "beautiful" has a third requirement: sensation must give rise to pleasure by engaging our capacities of reflective contemplation. Judgments of beauty are sensory, emotional, and intellectual all at once.

AESTHETICS IN FILM

Film combines many diverse disciplines, each of which may have its own rules of aesthetics. The aesthetics of cinematography are closely related to still photography, but the movement of the subject(s) or the camera and the intensities, colors, and placement of the lighting are highly important. Sound recording, editing, and mixing are other highly important areas of film, often closely related to the musical score. As in theatre, art direction in the design of the sets and shooting locations also applies, as does costume design and makeup. All of these disciplines are closely intertwined and must be brought together by the aesthetic sensibilities of the director.

PERFORMING ARTS AND AESTHETICS

Performing arts appeal to our aesthetics of storytelling, grace, balance, class, timing, strength, shock, humor, costume, irony, beauty, drama, suspense and sensuality. Whereas live stage performance is usually constrained by the physical reality at hand, film performance can further add the aesthetic elements of large-scale action, fantasy, and a complex interwoven musical score. Performance art often consciously mixes the aesthetics of several forms. Role-playing games are sometimes seen as a performing art with an aesthetic structure of their own, called RPG theory.

AESTHETIC JUDGMENT

Aesthetic judgment is a philosophy that questions the legitimacy of people's notions of what is pleasing to their tastes. Early puritanical thought equated beauty with pleasure, and pleasure was seen as evil. As the idea of aesthetic judgment evolved, it became the consensus that one should not like something because it was pleasurable to their senses but that like of something should be supported by one's ability to reconcile that object with the tools of their education and knowledge. Philosopher Immanuel Kant proposed that beauty should be judged both for its subjectivity and universality. Scottish philosopher David Hume also published a series of works on the validity of aesthetic judgment. In his essay on the aesthetic of tragedy, he explained that tragedy could be a pleasurable experience because even though it provokes a sense of sadness, it also produces a sense of delight in the viewing of a theatrical production. In such cases, Hume claims, the conflicting emotions of pleasure and displeasure are balanced by each other and balanced emotion results in pleasure.

Chapter Quiz

Ready to see how well you retained what you just read? Scan the QR code to go directly to the chapter quiz interface for this study guide. If you're using a computer, simply visit the online resources page at **mometrix.com/resources719/nystcetheater166** and click the Chapter Quizzes link.

Pedagogical Content Knowledge

Promoting Student Development of Theatre Concepts

Teaching Character Acting

The objective of a unit on character acting is to teach students how to develop, communicate and sustain characters in various performances. Students should learn to use sensory perception and emotional recall as tools to interpret and enact characters. They should learn how to recognize differences in characters and how to use their imaginations to create and show the thoughts and emotions of a character. Students should learn how characters can be used to develop situations in both individual and collaborative works. Students should develop skills in acting analysis as well as become familiar with improvisational skills. Students should be taught how to use vocal techniques in character portrayal and how to use movement to convey a character's thoughts and feelings. Character acting units should also include lessons on how technical elements of theatre can be used to enhance characterizations.

Gauging Students' Progress

Beginning level: At a beginner's level, students should be capable of using physical, emotional and social elements to portray a character in monologues, duets and improvised scenes. They should be capable of recreating a character through observation. Beginning students should have the ability to use their imaginations to improvise a character's thoughts and emotions and should be able to use improvisational skills to create a character. Students should be able to demonstrate an understanding of how vocal techniques are used to control volume and clarity when speaking. They should be able to distinguish between the various styles of acting as well as to identify ways to analyze characters. Beginning students should have an understanding of how technical elements like costume, makeup, props and lighting can enhance character development. Beginning students should be able to demonstrate through improvised scenes how movement can be used to express the thoughts and emotions of characters.

Intermediate level: Intermediate-level students should be capable of incorporating physical, emotional and social elements into their portrayal of individual characters. They should be able to create characters based on analysis of a script and to develop characters from the thoughts and feelings expressed in script dialogue. Students should have the ability to use improvisational skills when acting. Intermediate students should also have the ability to use analytical skills to develop characters in scripted scenes and to use movement to express thoughts and feelings in scripted scenes. Students should have the ability to use various styles of acting to portray characters. Intermediate students should be able to incorporate technical elements like costume, makeup, props and lighting to enhance characters.

Advanced level: Advanced students should be able to develop, communicate and sustain a character for the duration of a published script. They should have an ability to incorporate physical, social and emotional elements while portraying characters. The advanced student can create characterizations using complete scripts and can use imagination to develop a character's thoughts and emotions based on the dialogue and relationships within the script. Advanced students can use improvisational skills to create complex characters. They should be able to develop and analyze various approaches to characterizations and to determine the effectiveness of certain approaches as they are used in full-length scripts. Advanced students should show proficiency in selecting and applying technical elements to specific characters in full-length productions. They should be capable of using the vocal techniques implied in a script. Advanced students should have the ability to perform in ensembles while utilizing movement to convey thoughts, feelings and character.

Teaching Script Analysis

In a basic unit on script analysis geared toward 9th-12th grade students, the lessons should teach students how to improvise, write and edit scripts. The students should learn the principles of script writing and must be taught how to examine their own life experiences as well as how to create imaginary situations that can then be used in script writing. Students should be instructed as to how to use proper vocabulary involving meaning, character and subtext when writing a script. Students should have an understanding of the technical elements of theatre when writing a script. A unit on script analysis should also contain instruction on methods of developing and resolving dramatic problems. Upon completion, students should be able to demonstrate a basic understanding of people and life situations and how these can be used in a script.

Gauging Students' Progress

At the most basic level, a student who studies script writing should be capable of writing alone or with others. A student should be able to write original scenarios as well as create various characters, incorporating the appropriate literary elements and devices into the writing. The student should be able to identify dramatic situations, stage directions, technical notations and colloquial dialogues or subtext in published literature. In addition to being able to use the knowledge from the beginning level, the intermediate level student must be able to create multiple characters and settings and incorporate them into a complete scene containing a clear beginning, middle and end. Intermediate students should be capable of using colloquial dialogue and including stage directions and technical notations in their own writing. Advanced students should be able to create complex characters. They should have the ability to create a script in the appropriate format, which contains dynamic and dramatic situations, plot and development, colloquial dialogue and subtext and well-developed characters.

Teaching Stage Direction

When introducing students to theatre, it is important to provide them with the proper vocabulary tools. For example, students could be placed in groups of three to five and instructed to draw or sketch a stage set and then describe in writing the set they create. This written description would allow students to utilize any existing knowledge they have of stage direction while discovering the difficulty of conveying stage descriptions without the proper terminology. Once the activity is completed, the proper vocabulary terms are introduced. These include upstage, downstage, stage right, stage left and center stage, which are then explained in relation to how they are used in scripts and by actors and directors. This activity can be brought to life by using the classroom as a stage and having students move to the area that matches the name they call out. This lesson can be taken to a higher level by providing scripts in which the stage directions have been omitted and instructing students to provide their own stage direction based on the actions in the play.

Teaching Scene Design

It is important for theatre students to understand the importance of scene design in both formal and informal productions. Students should learn to conceptually design and technically produce scene design through various exercises and projects. Lessons involving scene design should cover the terminology, techniques and materials used in theatre performances. The students should gain an understanding of the various roles in theatre management. Lessons should examine theatre design and teach students how to analyze scene design in various types of productions. Lessons should explore scene design as a profession while including activities that allow students to actively participate in the development and production of scene design. Students should be given the opportunity to participate in scene design in order to determine their aptitude and inclination to pursue this particular niche in the future.

Gauging Students' Progress

Beginning level: Students who have taken only one theatre class are considered beginners. After completing a unit on scene design, beginning students should be able to identify both the technical and managerial elements involved in creating theatrical and dramatic effects for performances. They should be able to demonstrate their knowledge by taking on various roles or responsibilities in a dramatic performance. Students should understand the roles and responsibilities involved in theatre management including box office, advertising and house management. Beginning students should be able to demonstrate their knowledge of scene design, costume, sound, lighting and props. They should also understand and be able to demonstrate their knowledge of scene design as a profession and a hobby.

Intermediate level: Intermediate-level theatre students will have had two to three years of theatre classes. They should have the ability to create technical designs as well as theatre management designs. Intermediate students should have the ability to collaborate with a group to perform various technical and managerial roles and responsibilities. Students at this level should have the ability to apply their knowledge by participating in tasks involved with advertising, house management and box office duties. At this level, students should participate in various design positions in a theatre performance and should be able to distinguish between the possibility of pursuing theatre scene design as a hobby or as a profession.

Advanced level: Advance students have taken three or four years of theatre classes. Advanced students should be able to apply their knowledge by creating technical and theatre management designs for full-length dramatic productions. Advanced students should be capable of managing and supervising a technical crew or staff. They should be capable of demonstrating leadership abilities by organizing and overseeing a staff that is responsible for the various tasks involved in theatre management. Advanced students must be able to analyze, design and execute the requirements for any given design element in any type of production. Advanced students should actively participate in various theatre positions in order to assess their own aptitude and inclination to pursue those roles in either a professional or a vocational capacity.

Teaching Directing

During a unit on theatrical directing, students should learn to interpret scripts, conduct rehearsals and organize theatre productions. Students should receive instruction on how to analyze a dramatic text to determine production value. They should learn how to solve acting and technical problems as well as how to evaluate the suitability of various solutions. Lessons should provide students the opportunity to develop leadership skills through directing both formal and informal productions. Students should also have the chance to develop collaborative skills by working in groups to direct and produce performances. The functions and responsibilities of directors should be covered in the lessons. Students should also gain an understanding of the principles and importance of stage movement.

Gauging Students' Progress

Beginning level: Students at a beginning level should be familiar with the role of a director and be able to identify a director's responsibilities. Students should be capable of working alone or in groups to demonstrate the leadership and collaborative skills used by a director when creating a production. Students should be able to read a script, identifying potential problems that a director might face and should be able to propose solutions to those problems. Students should be capable of demonstrating their knowledge of stage movement, including blocking and choreography. Students at a beginning level should also be familiar with the historical timelines and trends related to directing.

Intermediate and advanced levels: Students who have taken two to three years of theatre classes are considered to be at the intermediate level. These students should be capable of performing the role of a director in a short scene. They should be able to work alone and in a group, easily conveying leadership and collaborative skills through directing short productions and one-act performances. Once intermediate students have directed a short or one-act piece, they should be able to identify problems in the directing process and creatively find solutions to those problems. Intermediate students should demonstrate the ability to incorporate the appropriate stage movement in a scene that they are directing. Advanced students who have taken theatre for three or four years should be able to fully direct an ensemble performance while integrating the proper stage movement into the performance. They should also be capable of anticipating problems and be able to quickly resolve unforeseen problems that might arise while directing.

Teaching History of Theatre

During a unit on the history of theatre, students should learn to research and evaluate the origins of theatre. They should learn to recognize the characteristics of various genres, eras and styles of theatre. They should be able to understand and discuss the contributions made to theatre by historical figures in each era and theatre style. Students should grasp how the culture, religion and politics of each geographical area affected the development of theatre and have an understanding of the social impact that theatre itself has made. They should be able to recognize and name the works and authors that dominated each genre and era of theatre. Students should also be able to discuss significant figures in the history of theatre and the contributions they made in the areas of acting, scene design, script analysis, lighting, sound, special effects, directing and theatrical management.

Teaching Theatrical Presentation

Theatrical presentation should involve familiarizing students with the broad range of activities that can be considered theatrical forms, which include music, dance, performance and visual arts. Students should examine the structure of dramatic productions and understand how that structure is the underlying form of all arts. They should be able to create a performance that integrates knowledge of various forms of theatre. Lessons should provide a means for students to study both traditional and non-traditional methods of artistic production. This should include hands-on experience in emerging technology in theatrical productions including film, video and computer.

Teaching Scene Comprehension

Theatre students should receive formal instruction on scene comprehension. Scene comprehension consists of the ability to analyze, critique, and infer meaning from various theatrical productions. Students should be exposed to several productions including both formal and informal performances. Students can exercise comprehension by viewing musical performances, dramatic productions, television and film. By critiquing these performances, students can gain an understanding of how to interpret and analyze productions, as well as understand the role played by the audience. Students should learn how the audience can be incorporated into various types of productions and should be introduced to methods of judging the aesthetic quality of a performance. They should learn to compare and contrast various performances in order to analyze the effectiveness of delivery.

Indicators of Proficient Students

Proficient students can use theatre vocabulary to describe theatrical experiences. They are able to collaborate with other theatre students and participate in a theatrical production in any related capacity. Students are able to recognize subtext, symbolism and metaphors in scripts and performances. Creatively, proficient students are able to create characters using script analysis, research and imagination. They can also utilize their knowledge to make acting decisions during rehearsals. Students can write dialogue and scenes that employ dramatic structure and should be able to design, produce and perform plays that demonstrate their comprehension of various theatrical styles and historical periods.

Indicators of Advanced Students

Advanced students should demonstrate the ability to creatively develop characters from a variety of dramatic texts, both realistic and fictional. They should have the skills to research, reflect and revise their acting choices for various characters. Advanced students should be able to use dialogue to advance action when writing a script. They should also be able to utilize the basic dramatic structure while writing a script and to develop complex characters to populate the script. In regards to understanding the historical aspects of theatre, advanced students should be able to research and perform a particular historical or cultural piece while using the appropriate dialect and mannerisms throughout the performance. Advanced students should understand the way the impact that theatre has and continues to have on society and culture. Students should also be capable of designing, performing and directing plays that are representational of specific theatrical styles. Advanced students should be able to use the appropriate vocabulary terms to discuss their aesthetic judgments of dramatic works.

Important Terms

Dramatic Performance Terms

Acting process: this term refers to the methods and materials from which an actor draws the ability to perform. Actors should be able to verbalize the tools they use in their acting processes.

Affective memory: a technique in which an actor reactivates a past experience to gain the emotional and psychological feelings associated with those events and then transfer them to a performance; used when the actor believes the character they are portraying is undergoing an event that emotionally parallels that which the actor has experienced in real life.

Atmosphere: defined by Michael Chekhov as the inherent energy within a specific place. Actors may imagine they are in a specific location while performing in order to depict the corresponding emotions and actions that would best suit that environment, thus creating an atmosphere.

Character acting occurs when an actor must make a change to their physical person in order to perform a role. This may include the use of dialect or accents that are not part of the actor's real persona or using stage makeup to create a specific facial disfigurement.

Career Opportunities in Theatre

Career Opportunities Available in Theatre and the Entertainment Industry

Within the theatre and entertainment industry, there are four types of roles: creative, production-related, service-related, and administration related. **Creative roles** are those that in some way apply their creative skills to the production. This can include costume designers, choreographers, playwriters, theater directors, and performers. **Production-related** roles address technical, behind-the-scenes aspects of productions. Sound and lighting technicians, set builders, casting directors, and producers fall under this category. **Service related** roles are customer facing positions and are usually front of house or management staff. Some examples include ticket sales, management positions, and ushers. **Administration related** roles encompass agents, teachers and instructors, marketers, and human relations. While theatre is often seen as performer focused, it takes a variety of roles to put on a production.

Types of Advanced Educational Opportunities Available in the Field of Theatre

As in many other professions, continuing and advanced educational opportunities allow theatre professionals to continue working on and improving their practice. Many universities offer undergraduate, graduate, and doctoral programs in theatre arts and performance studies. These are paths for performers and production-related roles. Playwriters can pursue higher studies in writing through similar programs. More specialized roles like choreographers and costume designers should pursue opportunities aligned with their craft. Outside of higher education courses, there are often workshops, seminars, and craft classes offered that provide a focused objective in a shorter amount of time. Joining guilds and professional organizations provides access to these opportunities for members.

Reputable Theatre Organizations

There are a variety of theatre organizations that work towards different goals. The following are well known organizations in the theatre community.

- Actor's Equity Association (AEA): AEA is a union for actors and stage managers. They work to protect the rights and advocate for the career advancements of members.
- American Society for Theatre Research (ASTR): ASTR provides a platform for scholarship of theatre and to help theatre groups connect. They provide awards, grants, and prizes in theatre.
- American Theatre Drama Society (ATDS): ATDS is dedicated to the study and history of drama in the Americas. They provide members with opportunities for study and travel.
- Dramatists Guild of America (DGA): DGA focuses on playwrights, composers, lyricists, and librettists. They work to ensure fair and ethical practices in the aforementioned fields.
- Black Theatre Network (BTN): BTN works to explore and preserve African related theatre. They provide a platform for communication and information within the black theatre community.

Contents of Popular Theatre and Trade Publications

- **American Theatre Magazine** is America's only general theatre magazine. It covers up and coming artists and performers, trends, and the economy as it relates to theatre.
- **Theatre Journal** is a quarterly collection of scholarly articles and reviews for the theatre community.
- **The Drama Review**, also known as TDR, is an academic journal that studies social, economic, aesthetic, and political contexts of productions.
- **New Theatre Quarterly** is a publication of peer-reviewed journals about theatre studies.
- **Journal of Dramatic Theory and Criticism** distributes full length articles that focus on a variety of drama related content.
- **New England Theatre Journal** covers a broad range of theatre topics including pedagogy, performance theory, theatre design, and related technology.

Theatre Instruction

Incorporating Theater in Elementary School

First Grade

In the first grade, students can be exposed to various forms of theatre. They can gain knowledge of the theatre by viewing formal, informal, video and television productions. The goal is to teach children how to process, analyze and respond to sensory information that is unique to theatre. First grade students can be taught the skills of artistic perception through lessons involving basic comprehension of theatre and its vocabulary. Creative expression can be cultivated by performing improvisational and pantomime activities. These students may also dramatize fictional and real-life stories to demonstrate a plot structure containing a beginning, middle and end. They can learn to identify the history and culture of theatre by understanding the geographical origins of a story. In first grade, students should be allowed to develop aesthetic judgment by expressing their emotional reactions to various forms of theatre.

Second Grade

Students should be taught about artistic perception through activities and lessons that utilize theatre vocabulary. Students should have the opportunity to demonstrate an understanding of artistic perception by acting out alternative endings to stories. Second grade students should be taught creative expression through activities that allow them to perform in groups to build cooperation skills. They can be taught how to pantomime concepts like hunger, anger, friendship and excitement. With regards to theatre history and context, students can be taught to identify stories from different cultures as well as identify universal character-types. Aesthetic judgment can be developed by allowing students to recognize and critique an actor's performance with regard to the actor's use of voice, movement and gesture. By second grade, students should have the ability to identify the moral of a story.

Third Grade

In third grade, students are further exposed to artistic perception through lessons on theatre vocabulary. They should also be taught to identify the five basic elements of a story: who, what, where, when and why (the "Five Ws"). Creative expression can be developed by allowing students to work together to write a script that uses the Five Ws. They should also be able to demonstrate knowledge of stage direction by writing a script that uses basic blocking. Historical aspects of theatre can be taught by allowing students to perform different versions of similar stories from around the world. Students in the third grade should be able to identify universal themes in stories and can be taught aesthetic judgment by developing and applying criteria to judge the success or quality of a performance. These students should also be able to compare the content and messages contained in two separate works.

Fourth Grade

Students in the fourth grade should continue expanding their theatre vocabulary. They should also build upon their existing knowledge of artistic perspective by learning to identify a character's motives. Students should learn how subtle changes in voice can be used to convey meaning during speaking and acting. The use of artistic expression should be cultivated by participation in activities where the students must express the emotions of actors through use of gestures. They should also retell stories in various tones, including comic and tragic. Students should have the opportunity to create a character through use of costumes, masks and props. Regarding the history of theatre, students should be introduced to local theatre history and trends. Their aesthetic judgment abilities should be developed by critiquing performances based on the elements of acting they have studied.

They should also understand the audience's impact on various types of performances. Fourth grade students should be able to view a dramatic performance and identify the methods employed by the scriptwriter to evoke a certain response from the audience.

Fifth Grade

Students in the fifth grade should develop artistic perception through the use of theatrical vocabulary in descriptions of theatrical experiences. The students should be taught to identify the structural elements of plot in scripts and performances. This includes exposition, complication, crisis, climax and resolution. Students should be allowed to develop their creative expression abilities through participation in improvisational activities examining universal themes. Students should also understand the concepts of blocking in theatre. The students should be further allowed to develop their creativity by participating in an actual performance where they perform the duties of an actor, director, writer or technical assistant. In regards to teaching the historical and cultural aspects of theatre, students should be allowed to make costumes, sets and props for a cultural celebration. Students should also examine cultural traditions and beliefs as they are reflected in the stories and plays of various cultures. In regards to the aesthetic element, students should evaluate the methods used by actors to convey meaning in their performances.

Incorporating Theater in Secondary Schools

Sixth Grade

Students in the sixth grade should continue to learn and to use theatre vocabulary. Artistic perception is taught through lessons that involve the importance of production value. Creative expression can be developed by having students participate in performances that demonstrate their knowledge of text, context and subtext. Students should utilize facial expression, voice, gestures and timing in a performance to convey the essence of the character they are playing. Creativity can be further developed by having students write a play that uses monologues, dialogues, actions, settings and a multitude of characters. Students should be asked to create a script that demonstrates their knowledge of a specific culture or historical period. They should also study theatrical traditions and histories on a global level. Sixth grade students should be able to aesthetically judge a theatrical experience by taking into consideration the quality and effectiveness of lighting, sets, costume, makeup and props. Students should also understand how theatre, television, film, politics and culture can interact and influence each other.

Seventh Grade

Students in the seventh grade should be introduced to more theatre vocabulary. They should develop the ability to identify dramatic elements including foreshadowing, crisis, rising action, catharsis and denouement. In order to develop skills in creative expression students should be allowed to explore character and motivation by participating in rehearsals. They should learn the value of maintaining a rehearsal script in order to organize their rehearsal time and to keep track of their thoughts and ideas concerning blocking, props and lighting. Students should be taught to incorporate tension and suspense into their writing. Regarding the historical and cultural aspects of theatre, student should participate in a culture-specific performance where they design and create the masks, costumes and sets. Students should also be able to compare and contrast various theatrical styles. With regard to aesthetic judgment, students should understand how cultural influences affect the content and meaning of drama.

Eighth Grade

In the eighth grade, students should continue to develop theatre vocabulary. They should learn to identify recurring themes, such as loyalty and revenge, in scripts and performances. Students should explore the use of figurative language and imagery in various dramatic works. With regard to creative expression, students should create short performances that target a specific genre or style of theatre, such as vaudeville and melodrama. Students should also participate in improvisational activities in which they use voice, blocking, monologue and pantomime to covey meaning in their character. Students should understand how American history is and was reflected in various styles of theatre, such as minstrel shows and musicals. Students should also be able to identify how technology has changed theatre over time. In order to develop skills in aesthetic judgment, students should write a full review of a dramatic production. They should also be able to identify similar plots and themes occurring in differing theatrical styles and cultures.

Applying Theater Lessons to Other Subject Areas

In first grade, students learn to cooperate in group activities. They also begin to understand the concept that, like a story, all things in life have a beginning, middle and an end. In second grade students learn problem-solving skills, which can be carried into other courses. By the third grade, students learn to question events and gain information through applying the five Ws (who, what, when, where and why). In fourth grade students learn to use acting as a tool to understand local history. They also learn to identify with a team in order to accomplish a specific goal. In fifth grade students learn about the various career options available to professional actors and theatrical technicians. In sixth grade student learn how theatrical skills are used in social sciences, such as advertising and marketing and in seventh grade they learn how voice can be used to project confidence during oral presentations. In eighth grade students begin to understand the various jobs available in theatre and they learn to research the educational requirements necessary for those jobs.

Relationship Between Art, Music, and Literature

Art and music contain many opportunities for interacting with literature for the enrichment of all. Students could apply their knowledge of art and music by creating illustrations for a work or creating a musical score for a text. Students could discuss the meanings of texts and decide on their illustrations, or a score could amplify the meaning of the text. Understanding the art and music of a period can make the experience of literature a richer, more rewarding experience. Students should be encouraged to use the knowledge of art and music to illuminate the text. Examining examples of dress, architecture, music, and dance of a period may be helpful in a fuller engagement of the text. Much of period literature lends itself to the analysis of the prevailing taste in art and music of an era, which helps place the literary work in a more meaningful context.

Trade Books

Some educators say stories about heroes serve as a source for teaching values. Some studies indicate recent trends on teaching values in connection with methods of analysis. Personal models such as heroes in history, fiction, and current events help to exemplify and encourage emulation of certain virtues or desirable traits of character such as civility, courage, honesty, perseverance, self-restraint, compassion, and fairness, as well as respect for the dignity of individuals and responsibility for the common good. Trade books are a good source for using heroes to teach values. These stories should be accurate and present both positive and negative aspect of a person's life. Multimedia instruction, including the use of videotapes, can help add depth to the portrayal.

Benefits of Theatre Program in Elementary or Secondary Schools

Schools that provide theatre programs and classes can benefit students by increasing critical and creative thinking. Theatre programs can help students to develop problem-solving skills as well as help students become effective communicators. Students learn how to collaborate with others and to coordinate their individual skills within a group. They learn planning and implementation skills, as well as how to research using libraries, computers and living sources. Students in theater programs can gain a greater understanding of cultural and historical events and beliefs. These students have the opportunity to develop a high-level of self-awareness as well as to increase self-confidence and become more socially aware.

THEATRE CURRICULUM IN SECONDARY EDUCATION

Teaching theatre in schools is often seen as unnecessary and disruptive to the educational curriculum, but studies have shown that theatre classes can offer many benefits to students. Theatre classes help to develop emotional intelligence, an everyday skill that is crucial in developing relationships and making life choices. Schools that neglect to incorporate a theatre component in the curriculum risk sending some of their students into the world not fully equipped with the emotional intelligence they will need in life. Author Reed Larson's study, published in the journal Child Development, explains that through a study conducted in an Illinois high school he observed that students who were taking a theatre class had much more positive emotional experiences than those who were not taking a theatre class. Larson believes that theatre class helps students learn how to constructively work through emotions rather than to react negatively in stressful or frustrating situations. Additionally, the theatre students in Larson's study were described as better able to help other students master a higher degree of emotional intelligence.

COURSE DESCRIPTION

Students in high school theatre arts courses will study, write, research, critique, create, design, perform and participate in a variety of theatre-based learning experiences. Three levels of instruction will be included, allowing for a total of four years of theatre arts classes. The courses will include instruction in performance and design techniques, style, historical motifs and genres, creating performance-based experiences while using appropriate technology and media. These courses will develop critical thinking, creativity and aesthetic perception and will reinforce skills in leadership and collaboration. The program of study will generate a heightened sensitivity to the arts and will explore theatre's significance and influence on society.

Chapter Quiz

Ready to see how well you retained what you just read? Scan the QR code to go directly to the chapter quiz interface for this study guide. If you're using a computer, simply visit the online resources page at **mometrix.com/resources719/nystcetheater166** and click the Chapter Quizzes link.

NYSTCE Practice Test

Want to take this practice test in an online interactive format?
Check out the online resources page, which includes interactive practice questions and much more: **mometrix.com/resources719/nystcetheater166**

1. Which form of drama, also known as creative drama, involves an instructor guiding participants to first imitate actual experiences and then reflect upon them?

a. Product-centered drama
b. Process-centered drama
c. Natural-state drama
d. Method acting

2. Theatre in Education, or TIE, is considered a mix of formal theatre and creative drama (also known as process-centered drama) where the outcome of a performance:

a. Is undetermined and solely at the discretion of performers "in the moment"
b. Is scripted, meaning actors are limited by specific dialog and movements
c. Has various versions that the performers must choose *before* performing
d. Is completely up to the teacher

3. A high school drama class is studying the play *Huckleberry Finn.* The teacher asks two students to get in front of the class and act out the roles of Huck Finn and Tom Sawyer. However, she asks the students to rely on their imaginations and act as though Huck and Tom are 20 years older than they are in the actual play. This type of unscripted acting is called:

a. Spontaneous depiction
b. Improvisation
c. In-depth characterization
d. Character relationship analysis

4. If a drama teacher wanted to demonstrate pantomime to her students, she might do which of the following?

a. Recite Edgar Allen Poe's "The Raven"
b. Sing Evita's "Don't Cry for Me Argentina"
c. Sit cross-legged in the center of the room and chant
d. Attempt to tell a story using only facial expressions and bold gestures

5. A ninth-grade theatre class sits in a circle while their teacher lays a large rectangular piece of cloth in the center of the circle. Each student is asked to enter the circle, pick up the cloth, and answer the question: "What could this piece of fabric be?" The students are encouraged to use their imaginations while answering. This is an example of:

a. A theatre game used as a warm-up
b. Ad-libbing to create a plot
c. A concentration exercise
d. Skill development to encourage group cohesion

6. A fourth-grade drama teacher instructs two of her students to act out the following scenario using improvisation.

> You and your best friend are walking through a park and you find a diamond ring. You want to find the ring's rightful owner, but your friend insists on selling the ring for extra spending money.

This exercise is intended to aid in the class's comprehension of which of the following components of drama?

a. Conflict
b. Climax
c. Foreshadowing
d. Role reversal

7. What is the most important difference between process-centered drama and production-centered drama?

a. Production-centered drama always takes place on a main stage, while process-centered drama always takes place in a classroom.
b. Process-centered drama is free, while production-centered drama has many financial costs involved.
c. A teacher allows a high level of creative freedom in process-centered drama, whereas, in production-centered drama, there is a director, and the outcome is structured and predetermined.
d. Production-centered drama involves a high level of improvisation, whereas process-centered drama is entirely scripted.

8. Listening, reacting, engaging in eye contact, and thoroughly understanding prompts are all useful elements when nurturing a student's ability to develop what broad skill?

a. Effective interaction
b. Performance
c. Rehearsal
d. Role playing

Refer to the following for questions 9–10:

A drama teacher has a class with students of diverse backgrounds. He noticed that some students appear uncomfortable in the class and don't seem to want to participate in group activities.

9. To encourage successful collaboration among members of an ensemble, the drama teacher must do all of the following EXCEPT:

a. Define performance goals
b. Involve all willing participants
c. Invite new ideas from the group
d. Force the group to make creative decisions without offering help

10. What should the drama teacher do to effectively educate the students of diverse backgrounds?

a. Seek out plays and scripts written by minorities
b. Single out students of diverse backgrounds and make them do oral reports on their culture
c. None of the answers are appropriate. It is never a drama teacher's responsibility to educate students about diversity
d. Assign minority roles to Caucasian students

11. Which of the following would be the most effective way for a director to create a sense of creative collaboration amongst his entire cast and crew before the rehearsal process begins?

a. He should take his cast members to a play so they can observe other actors before determining what type of actors they want to be
b. He should have a party so all cast members can get to know each other on a friendly basis
c. He should hold a table read-through of the script that involves every member of the ensemble, even those who have small parts
d. He should get cast members to do a simple warm-up that involves improvisation and theatre games

12. Which of the following is the most important aspect of writing or choosing a script for a third-grade classroom?

a. There needs to be a lesson learned at the end of the story.
b. The script must be appropriate for both the performer(s) and the audience.
c. The script must not call for expensive props.
d. The dialogue must not contain offensive language.

13. Fill in the blank: When critiquing students' monologues, it is important to help them through the refining process by ____:

a. Cutting content when their monologues are over five minutes in length
b. Rewriting and fine tuning verbiage so that all audience members can relate to the material
c. Encouraging them to stay in character for a full 24 hours to grasp the mood of the monologue
d. Making sure the student can identify with the character and is comfortable with the dialect and content

14. You ask each student in your fifth-grade drama class to close their eyes while you read a passage.

> A young girl walks along the beach with her dog as the waves tickle her feet. A boy approaches the girl and asks her if she would like to build a sandcastle with him.

Then, with their eyes opened, you ask each student to tell his or her own version of what happens next with the girl, the dog, and the boy on the beach. This is an example of using which source material?

a. Memory
b. Visualization
c. Imagination
d. Personal experiences

15. Fill in the blank: When reading or writing a script, character actions that occur while the character is speaking should appear in ____:

a. Upper case
b. Bold font
c. Parentheses
d. Brackets

16. An important script element of screenplay format that appears in all capital letters and tells the reader about the current scene setting is known as what?

a. Slug line
b. Header
c. Scene description
d. Theme

17. With respect to actor placement onstage, what does the term "upstage" mean?

a. The actor is toward the back of the stage, away from the audience.
b. The actor is positioned at the front of the stage, close to the audience.
c. The actor is exactly at the center of the stage.
d. The actor is standing on an X on the stage that was put in place by the director.

18. A second-grade teacher divides half of her class into three groups and assigns a room (bathroom, kitchen, dining room, etc.) to each group. Each student picks an item or utensil that is vital to their assigned room. One student chooses a refrigerator, another chooses a mirror, another chooses a fork, etc. They are not allowed to say which item they chose aloud. The teacher picks a student and says, "I'm going to have a garage sale, and I'm going to put you up for sale." The student responds by saying, "No! You can't sell me." The student goes on to explain why the room he is standing in cannot function without him. If he picked a refrigerator, for example, he might say, "Your food would go rotten without me!" The other half of the class has to figure out which room the students are standing in based on their responses. This theatre game not only uses improvisation, but also teaches students:

a. Critical thinking skills
b. Imagery
c. Prop placement
d. Collaboration

19. Mood and setting can often be confused with one another. What is the main distinction between the two terms?

a. Mood is created solely by the characters and their actions. Setting is the physical location of the play
b. Sensory details determine the mood, allowing the audience to feel certain emotions. Setting is what the audience sees in terms of set design
c. Mood is created by a lighting designer, while setting is created by a set designer
d. Setting is entirely dependent on the mood. They cannot exist without one another

20. Fill in the blank: A common form of storytelling that involves manipulating inanimate objects to make them look like living beings is known as ____:

a. Puppetry
b. Pantomime
c. Make-believe
d. Animation

21. Finish the following sentence by selecting the best answer choice. Visiting your local library, joining theatre organizations, researching theatre topics online, and networking with fellow drama teachers are all ways to:

a. Enhance social skills, which are extremely important for drama teachers
b. Utilize professional source materials
c. Increase your chances of getting a lead role in a community play
d. Complete a continuing education credit

22. All of the following are examples of widely studied ancient theatre forms except:

a. Greek.
b. Roman
c. English Renaissance
d. Medieval

23. Which of the following was a unique aspect of classical Greek theatre that set it apart from other genres?

a. Actors never spoke on stage
b. Performances utilized just three actors onstage
c. Greek theatres were very small, and could hold just 20 audience members at a time
d. Greek actors were the first to incorporate puppetry into performances

24. What is *Commedia dell'Arte* and where did it originate?

a. It is a physical, comical type of acting that broke through language barriers. It originated in Italy
b. It is slapstick humor that uses gestures instead of spoken words. It originated in Belgium
c. It is dark humor and sarcasm. It originated in America
d. It is pantomime that uses music to tell a story. It originated in Moscow

25. The English Renaissance is a time period most known for its:

a. Operas
b. Comedians
c. Playwrights
d. Classical musicians

26. Method acting emerged in 20th century America with the help of Russian performer Constantin Stanislavski. All of the following are requirements of method acting except:

a. Patience
b. Skilled listening
c. Astute focus
d. Sense of humor

27. A seventh-grade drama teacher asks his students to close their eyes and think of their favorite cookies right out of the oven. He asks, "How does the smell of the cookies affect you?" The teacher then asks the students to perform an impromptu scene from grandma's house. Which technique did the drama teacher use?

a. Sensory recall
b. Focus
c. Perception
d. Characterization

28. According to Richard Boleslavsky, author of *Acting: The First Six Lessons,* a performer must hone certain skills to become successful. He stresses education of the body, education of the mind, and development of the soul. These are components of which type of acting?

a. Practical aesthetics
b. Meisner technique
c. Method acting
d. Active analysis

29. Analyzing each character in a script, studying biographical information, and understanding each characters' strengths and weaknesses are important aspects of:

a. Developing character relationships
b. Script analysis
c. Plot development
d. Psychological dissection

30. An eighth-grade theatre teacher asks her class to inhale by yawning, and then let out all the air by sighing as loudly as possible. This is an example of:

a. Vocal projection
b. Pitch development
c. Vocal warm-up
d. Breath control

31. A vocal teacher instructs his students to sing "Mary Had a Little Lamb" without consonants, stressing only the vowels. He asks his students to be aware of what shapes their mouths make during this exercise. This is an example of practicing:

a. Diction
b. Tempo
c. Phrasing
d. Tone

32. The forceful vocal projection that occurs when a performer uses her chest instead of her diaphragm while breathing will most likely result in:

a. A lower pitch
b. Vocal injury
c. A higher pitch
d. Loss of vocal control

33. Two commonly misused terms in theatre are pitch and tone. Choose the answer that best describes the difference between the two terms.

a. Tone is the actual value of a note (B sharp, for example). Pitch is sound quality
b. There is no difference between the two terms. They are interchangeable
c. Pitch is the value of the note (C flat, for example). Tone measures the quality of the note's sound
d. Pitch is the value of a note sung by a performer. Tone is the value of a note played on a musical instrument

34. Choose the answer that best finishes the following sentence. A neutral mask is ____:

a. Without color
b. Made of organic materials
c. Without expression
d. Always flesh-colored

35. If a drama teacher wanted to deepen his students' understanding of human emotions and characterization, he might bring which of the following to class?

a. Costumes
b. Commedia half-masks
c. Comedy/tragedy masks
d. Character masks

36. Charlie is playing the villain in his high school play. Before going onstage for his scene, he shakes his fist in the air to trigger the evil essence of his character. While he is onstage, his evil act starts to fade, so he envisions himself shaking his fist in order to recapture the nature of his character. This tactic is called:

a. Psychological gesture
b. Character conceptualization
c. Mental movement
d. Chekhov method

37. The director of a production has many duties. All of the following are assumed duties of a director except:

a. Vocal coaching
b. Encouraging cohesion among cast mates
c. Interpreting and approving scripts
d. Collaborating with crew members

38. A middle school theatre teacher finds a script that he is very passionate about for his seventh graders to perform. The only problem with the script is that it contains language that is inappropriate not only for his students, but also for the audience. Assuming permission to alter the script is not obtained, which of the following would be the best course of action for the teacher?

a. Find a completely new script for the seventh graders
b. Omit the foul words from the script, but leave the plot line as is
c. Have the students rewrite the script in their own words
d. Leave the script as is so the original playwright won't be upset

39. A director asks his entire company to form a circle, and then asks that cast members stand between crew members. Everyone is then directed to turn to their right so they are facing the back of the person standing next to them. On the director's count of three, everyone is to sit in the lap of the person behind them. If everyone does this correctly, the company will form a self-sustaining "chair circle." What is the director trying to create through this activity?

a. A positive working environment for his cast and crew
b. Distinction between crew members and actors
c. Efficiency and productivity
d. Competition between crew members and actors

40. A director is having a difficult time keeping his company members motivated during rehearsals. Rehearsals are four hours in length and will continue for another three weeks. Which of the following would be the most effective tactic to employ in this situation?

a. The director should give the cast one week off from rehearsals
b. The director should collaborate with his cast to decide on a break time
c. The director should force the cast to have dinner together after rehearsals
d. The director should shorten rehearsals to two hours instead of four

41. To ensure maximum dramatic effect, a director places actors onstage precisely where he wants them. What is this called?

a. Positioning
b. Staging
c. Choreography
d. Blocking

42. Drama teachers and directors often have to budget for theatrical performances. One main cost involved with putting on a production is purchasing scripts for cast members. It seems as though photocopying one script would be a logical way to cut costs. Why is photocopying scripts not a good idea?

a. Photocopying scripts without the permission of the playwright is considered copyright infringement, and could result in an expensive lawsuit
b. Scripts are so inexpensive that it costs less to purchase them than to buy the paper and ink needed to photocopy them
c. Script pages can get lost or shuffled around during photocopying
d. It is better for cast members to share scripts in order to collaborate with fellow cast mates

43. The character Hedy LaRue from *How to Succeed in Businesses Without Really Trying* is typically portrayed by a Caucasian woman. If a director wanted to cast an Asian American woman in his rendition of the play, what type of casting would this be?

a. Adverse casting
b. Diverse casting
c. Nontraditional casting
d. Curveball casting

44. When is a theatre production company required to pay royalty fees to a playwright for using his work?

a. On opening night
b. Every time admission is charged
c. Any time the play is performed for an audience
d. When the admission price exceeds five dollars per audience member

45. In order for a director to get an idea of a performer's capabilities and talent, he might ask the performer to read a script he or she has never seen before. This is called:

a. Blind reading
b. Preliminary reading
c. Sight-reading
d. Cold reading

46. A theatre director hoping to produce a low-cost series of experimental skits would benefit from using which type of theatrical stage?

a. Proscenium
b. Black box
c. Arena
d. Thrust

47. What is the difference between a thrust stage and an arena?

a. An audience can sit on three sides of a thrust stage; they can sit on all four sides of an arena.
b. A thrust stage cannot utilize a backstage, whereas an arena can.
c. An audience can only sit in front of a thrust stage; they can sit on three sides of an arena.
d. A thrust stage can be an unused room or warehouse converted into a theatre; an arena is also known as a platform stage.

48. A director might hire a dramaturg for what purpose?

a. To apply special effects makeup to the actors' faces and/or bodies
b. To analyze dramatic text and research relevant historical facts in order to determine the artistic requirements of a specific production
c. To incorporate lighting and sound effects to enhance the mood for the audience
d. To aid in marketing efforts and increase ticket sales

49. What is theatre gel used for?

a. It is a safety precaution in case someone gets burned by a stage light; theatre gel is applied to the skin to prevent scarring
b. Lighting technicians use theatre gels, or small transparent pieces of colored film, to change the mood with lighting
c. Sound technicians use theatre gels, or thick sound-resistant pads, to muffle sounds that are too loud
d. Costume designers use theatre gels, or adhesive liquids, to mend clothing when it tears or needs a quick hem

50. You are backstage and you see an electrical cable with sparks flying out of it. According to most theater safety rules and regulations, which of the following would be the most appropriate course of action?

a. Get some electrical tape and wrap it around the area where sparks are present.
b. Inform everyone on set and backstage so that a proper evacuation can take place.
c. Call the fire department.
d. Inform the stage manager or a lighting team member so they can assess the situation.

51. A document used by lighting designers and electricians that maps out exactly where each and every light bulb will be placed, which color will be used, and when they will be used is called what?

a. Light map
b. Lighting blue print
c. Lighting key
d. Light plot

52. A large instrument used for lighting that consists of a lamp socket and is surrounded by a reflector is called what?

a. A specific light
b. A general light
c. A strip light
d. A floodlight

53. When there are budget constraints, some directors and/or set designers will use a certain type of set that can be changed by merely adding one or two set pieces, which makes the set very versatile. What is this type of set called?

a. Unit set
b. Convertible set
c. Multi set
d. Uniform set

54. You were walking around barefoot backstage and cut your foot on an exposed nail. You find the first aid kit, clean the wound, and then put a bandage on your wound. What is the next course of action you should take?

a. Take the first aid kit to the local pharmacy so you can properly restock it for others to use
b. Put the first aid kit in its designated area immediately in case someone else needs it
c. Give it to your stage manager so she can restock it
d. Report your injury to the stage manager

55. As it relates to set design and scenery, a flat is:

a. A set that resembles a European apartment
b. A portion of flat scenery usually framed in wood and wrapped in canvas
c. A small piece of flat scenery hinged to another piece of flat scenery
d. A hinged metal plate used for suspending scenery

56. Fill in the blank: A batten can best be described as ____.

a. A long metal pole or pipe from which lighting, scenery, or curtains can be hung
b. A painted canvas or backcloth hung at the back of the stage
c. A hidden door in the stage where actors can enter and exit
d. A piece of cloth used to separate the stage from the audience

57. Costumes can help deepen the audience's understanding of a character's social status, gender, occupation, and personality through clothing and accessories. Costumes can also do which of the following?

a. Alter a performer's appearance
b. Distinguish relationships among characters
c. Convey changes in a character's age
d. All of the above

58. A chart that lists characters that will be onstage, what they will be wearing, and possible wardrobe difficulties for every scene is called what?

a. Costume plan
b. Costume sketch
c. Costume plot
d. Costume script

59. How do most high schools obtain costumes for theatrical productions?

a. High schools typically rent their costumes.
b. A costume designer makes the costumes.
c. Costumes are usually donated by students.
d. Costumes can be rented, made, or donated.

60. If a makeup designer needed an actor to appear older than he actually is, which of the following would be the best makeup technique to use?

a. After applying foundation to the face and neck, the makeup designer should highlight prominent facial muscles and darken the areas underneath the muscles
b. Before applying foundation to the face and neck, the makeup designer should highlight prominent facial muscles and darken the areas underneath the muscles
c. After applying foundation to the face and neck, the makeup designer should shade prominent facial muscles with dark tones and highlight the areas underneath the muscles
d. Before applying foundation to the face and neck, the makeup designer should shade prominent facial muscles with dark tones and highlight the areas underneath the muscles

61. A makeup designer must have a thorough understanding of physiognomy. What is the definition of physiognomy?

a. The practice of judging a person's character by studying his or her facial features
b. The study of human facial features
c. An understanding of facial neuroanatomy
d. The practice of massaging one's face for relaxation purposes

62. According to most manufacturers of theatrical makeup, cosmetic products contain preservatives. What is the purpose of these preservatives?

a. To prevent the transmission of infection due to makeup sharing
b. To prolong the shelf life of the product
c. To protect the product from color fading
d. To prevent discoloration under theatrical lighting

63. Foam urethane and latex are standard materials used for making:

a. Scenery backdrops
b. Simple prosthetics
c. Costume undergarments
d. Non-slip pads for actors' shoes

64. You have just been hired by a local theatre to ensure rehearsals go smoothly. Your duties include recording blocking, prop, and lighting aspects, as well as making sure performers stay on script. What is your job title?

a. Director
b. Crew manager
c. Technical director
d. Stage manager

65. Backstage etiquette and safety are vital to a production's success. All of the following answer choices are examples of backstage safety precautions that should be taken by crew members except:

a. Check all electrical cables and cords, making sure they are placed properly backstage so no one trips over them
b. Practice backstage procedures in light and dark conditions to become knowledgeable about set up and striking processes
c. Communicate with fellow crew members by using as few words as possible. Use code words if necessary to avoid lengthy conversations backstage
d. Practice striking in total darkness, which is important because the end of productions do not usually use lighting

66. Set construction, sound mixing and recording, light hanging, and prop procurement are all aspects of:

a. Process-centered theatre
b. Practical theatre
c. Technical theatre
d. Artistic theatre

67. One type of theatre borrowed many cultural aspects from Medieval theatre, including plays with religious undertones that were performed in European churches and secular festivals. Which historical type of theatre was it?

a. Renaissance
b. Neoclassical
c. Ancient Egyptian
d. Indian

68. Of the following works written by William Shakespeare, which one is considered a tragedy?

a. As You Like It
b. Macbeth
c. Henry VIII
d. A Lover's Complaint

69. Oscar Wilde (*The Importance of Being Earnest, Lady Windermere's Fan*) and George Bernard Shaw (*Pygmalion, Caesar and Cleopatra*) were both famous 19th century playwrights born in:

a. Ireland
b. France
c. Russia
d. England

70. Which genre of theatre pokes fun at current events and/or noteworthy people?

a. Farce
b. Comedy
c. Satire
d. Slapstick

71. A prime example of how live theatre has impacted society in the United States by creating jobs and attracting mass consumerism in a concentrated location is:

a. Broadway
b. West End
c. Experimental theatre
d. Comedy clubs

72. While most actors experience increases in confidence from performing in front of an audience, some individuals feel the negative emotional effects of theatre, which can include:

a. Paranoia
b. Claustrophobia
c. Performance anxiety
d. Mood swings

73. Which theatrical term best describes a dramatic outburst or a release of strong emotion by an actor or an audience member?

a. Catharsis
b. Alienation effect
c. Performance purification
d. Ablution

74. Bertolt Brecht was a famous playwright best known for coining a theatre technique that hinders an audience from relating too closely with characters so they can be observed from a more critical standpoint. What is this technique called?

a. Audience breach
b. Alienation effect
c. Dissension effect
d. Third-person effect

75. In order for someone writing a newspaper critique to give a theatre production a thorough evaluation, all of the following questions should be considered except:

a. What is the financial impact of the production on the community?
b. Did the lighting, set, and sound design help set the mood of the play?
c. Why exactly did the director choose to produce this particular play?
d. Which type of audience would most enjoy this production?

76. Publicity has a tremendous effect on how many people will view a particular production. Which of the following is the best way for a high school drama class to attract publicity for their play?

a. Create posters to display around the school and the community
b. Post the play's details (when, where, cost) on the school's website
c. Write and send press releases to the local newspaper
d. All of the above

77. What is the difference between a musical and an opera?

a. A musical is sung in English; an opera is sung in Italian.
b. Dance is typically incorporated in an opera; there is usually no dancing in musicals.
c. An opera is usually sung all the way through (without dialogue); musicals contain spoken dialogue between songs.
d. During an opera, a live orchestra fills the time between songs; during a musical, dance fills the time between songs.

78. There are two actors' onstage discussing politics. Tim reflexively rolls his eyes after Barry makes a comment. Barry responds to Tim's eye roll by saying, "Okay, clearly we need to change the subject." Barry's response was due to:

a. Vocal cues
b. Subtext
c. Script directions
d. Natural impulse

79. As an eighth-grade drama teacher, you discover that Kim is drawn to costume design, Theo has a knack for sound mixing, and Robert enjoys set design. You ask each student to write an essay describing the aspect of theatre he or she would like to explore. What does this encourage?

a. Self-evaluation
b. Self-discovery
c. Personal interpretation
d. Conformism

80. Choose the best answer to complete the following sentence. A theatre teacher should always encourage creative expression in the classroom unless ____:

a. It could be physically or emotionally harmful to students
b. A parent warns the teacher against it
c. It becomes motivational
d. It promotes collaboration among students

81. Which method would be the most appropriate for teaching sixth-grade students how to critique others' performances?

a. Conduct an open-ended conversation with anyone who wants to participate after a performance
b. After each act, encourage students to voice their opinions, good and bad
c. Instruct students to write down random thoughts about a performance while they are watching it
d. Before a performance, create a structured outline that includes the following headings: description, analysis, interpretation, and evaluation

82. Choose the answer that best completes the following sentences. Process-centered drama is most appropriate for ____; product-centered drama is most appropriate for ____

a. Very young students who need to learn self expression; older students exploring a structured theatre environment
b. Older students exploring a structured theatre environment; very young students who need to learn self expression
c. Students who want to explore the artistic side of theatre; students who want to explore the technical side of theatre
d. Girls; boys

83. Which situation would be an example of a junior high drama teacher using her knowledge of a student's prior experiences and interests to encourage participation and involvement in her classroom?

a. She asks the quarterback of the football team to play the lead in the popular play about baseball, *Damn Yankees*
b. She asks the shiest girl in class to sing a song of her choosing in front of the class
c. She asks the star of the baseball team to recite the poem, "Casey at the Bat"
d. She asks the class clown to play the very serious lead role in *The Crucible*

84. Although every audience is different, it is important to teach students audience etiquette. All of the following are universally appropriate rules to follow when attending a performance except:

a. Avoid speaking under all circumstances
b. Do not bring electronic gadgetry into a performance
c. Avoid falling asleep
d. Do not unwrap candy

85. Choose the answer that best completes the following sentences. Two seventh-grade drama students are given the opportunity to portray characters of their choosing. Tonya chooses to portray her great-great-grandmother, while Carlos chooses to portray Malcolm X. Tonya's character portrayal is drawn from ____; Carlos's character portrayal is drawn from ____.

a. History; current events
b. Heritage; history
c. Culture; diversity
d. Personal experience; literature

86. Students in a high school drama class are told to partner up and create an original script that is based on the personal experiences of both partners. This activity is designed to promote what?

a. A better understanding of interpersonal relationships
b. Creative problem solving
c. Self-confidence while performing in front of others
d. Exploration of content-related material

87. A class of third-graders watches as an onstage performer stomps her feet when she doesn't get what she wants. The third-graders understand that the actress is expressing anger because they have grasped the concept of:

a. Kinetics
b. Nonverbal communication
c. Gesturing
d. Body language

88. Which of the following would not be considered a professional developmental resource for a high school drama teacher?

a. Other theatre teachers
b. Community theatre actors
c. The World Wide Web
d. A local art museum

Answer Key and Explanations

1. B: Process-centered drama is the correct answer because this method of teaching is focused on a child's ability to play and act out what they see in actual life. It is more perception based, whereas product-centered drama focuses on teaching acting skills. It is more structured. Method acting is when a performer uses his thoughts and emotions to convey a message to the audience. A child cannot fully understand product-centered drama or method acting until he understands process-centered drama. Natural-state drama does not exist.

2. A: Theatre in Education could be considered the stepping stone that lies between process-centered drama and product-centered drama. Like process-centered drama, it is unscripted. The student who is introduced to TIE, however, should have a working knowledge of performing in front of peers. The key focus of Theatre in Education is to teach performers how to be "in the moment." A teacher or instructor can give initial guidance, but the outcome is determined by the student.

3. B: Because neither student in the example is familiar with Huck Finn or Tom Sawyer as adults, they have to use their imaginations and prior knowledge of the characters to create a whole new scenario. Answer choices C and D can be eliminated because the situation does not call for character or relationship analysis. A term that describes on-the-spot performing would be a better answer choice. The situation calls for spontaneity, so answer choice A might look correct. However, a better term for this type of performance is *improvisation.*

4. D: Pantomime is conveying a message without using speech through the use of body movements, facial expressions, or gestures. This question can be answered by using the process of elimination. Answer choices A, B, and C are all instances where the drama teacher uses her voice as a teaching method. Answer choice D, though, indicates that the teacher is using only gestures and expressions to tell a story. D is the correct answer choice.

5. A: Games are vital when educating young children about the art of theatre. Theatre games that stimulate the imagination are most likely to be warm-up exercises. Plot creation and concentration, which are mentioned in answer choices B and C, would come after the initial warm-up. The exercise does relate to group cohesion, which is mentioned in answer choice D, but the focus of the game is not interaction. Therefore, D is incorrect.

6. A: The situation clearly shows two different viewpoints. This difference creates conflict between the two friends. If the scenario described a situation where the two friends were working toward a resolution but the reader was still unaware of the consequences of their decision, (B) would be appropriate. Foreshadowing would have given hints as to where the story was headed, and role reversal is clearly not involved in this situation. Therefore, (C) and (D) are incorrect.

7. C: It is important to remember that process-centered drama involves an instructor encouraging his or her students to use their imaginations and reflect upon their own real-life experiences. Production-centered drama is much more structured and relies on predetermined outcomes. Here is an easy way to distinguish process-centered drama from production-centered drama: The words *process* and *recess* end in the same four letters. If a child is learning process-centered drama, they are most likely to also have recess or playtime, as this method is learned during the lower grades. Production-centered drama can be thought of as a grand, main-stage production with more mature actors.

8. A: Learning how to effectively interact with others is extremely important to a child's understanding of theatre. In order to fully grasp effective interaction, one must develop certain skills, such as listening, reacting, engaging in meaningful eye contact, and taking note of prompts from other performers. Performance, rehearsal, and role playing are great methods for honing interaction skills, but a student must understand the basic fundamentals of effective interaction before they can perform these activities.

9. D: In this question, look for the answer that does not belong. (A) through (C) suggest that the teacher is providing encouragement, while (D) does not. A drama teacher should never be reluctant to assist an ensemble with group decisions. An instructor should always be helpful and offer suggestions when asked. Collaboration can be difficult in a theatre setting since there are multiple people supplying input. It is a teacher's duty to involve everyone, encourage new ideas, and define goals as a group.

10. A: To effectively stress diversity in the classroom, a teacher should introduce scripts containing multicultural themes and characters of all ethnic backgrounds. It would never be a good idea to single out a student of a different race or cultural heritage for any reason, so (B) is incorrect. Teaching diversity is indeed part of most curriculums, so (C) is incorrect. Assigning minority roles to Caucasian students would be more closely related to nontraditional casting, not diversity in education, so (D) is incorrect.

11. C: All of the answer choices in this question would effectively create a sense of creative collaboration among cast members. However, there is one answer choice that is better than the others. The most important thing to keep in mind when encouraging collaboration is to include everyone. That means the cast members with small roles should feel just as important as those with the lead roles. This will create positive cohesion throughout the entire rehearsal process. Answer C is the best choice since it involves all cast members and focuses on the play that will be performed.

12. B: Plenty of third-grade-level scripts *do* contain lessons at the end of the story. Typically, though, only fables are supposed to include a moral lesson. Therefore, (A) is incorrect. If a script called for expensive props or contained offensive language, it would not be suitable to be performed by third-graders or to be viewed by an audience. Therefore, while both (C) and (D) are correct, (B) is the better choice because it is broader and encompasses both (C) and (D).

13. D: Performing a monologue can be unnerving for even the most experienced actor. When introducing young students to monologues, the most important thing to keep in mind is that they should feel comfortable with the content and dialect, and should be able to relate to the character in some way. Answer choices A through C are all good options when refining monologues, but establishing a comfort level between script and student is the most important aspect, making D the best choice.

14. C: The operative phrase in the question is *what happens next.* If the question called for a description, which would require students to use visualization skills, (B) would be the correct choice. The students most likely will use their memories and personal experiences as references in creating their stories, but because the teacher is asking *what's next,* the students have to use their imaginations more than anything else.

15. C: Action while a character is speaking should be identified with parentheses. If a character is not speaking, action is simply listed without special formatting. When formatting scripts, character names and headings appear in upper case letters while brackets are typically used to indicate offstage sounds. Bold text appears intermittently for highlighting names or important words.

16. A: A slug line (also called a scene heading) is a screenplay element written in all capital letters that establishes the scene's setting, including location and time of day. It should not be confused with other script elements such as headers or scene descriptions. Therefore, the correct answer is slug line.

17. A: There is an easy way to remember stage directions. There is an old wives' tale about stage construction that claims that stages used to be built on a slope (the back end was higher than the front). When a director wanted an actor to stand at the back of the stage, he literally meant, "Go *up* the stage." If the director wanted an actor positioned toward the front of the stage, he would say, "Go *down* the stage." Eventually, these directions were shortened to "upstage" and "downstage."

18. A: The children in this situation must apply critical thinking skills in order to successfully convey a message to the audience. They must *imagine* themselves in a specific room, *recall* which utensils or items belong in that room, and then take their thinking skills one step further by *deciding* why their item is necessary to the room. Answer choices B through D are not comprehensive enough to answer this question.

19. B: Mood relates to emotional responses. Audience members must use their senses to determine certain feelings, such as happiness, anger, sadness, and confusion. The director can evoke certain emotions through set design, costuming, and lighting choices. Setting can help determine mood. However, setting is concrete, as it is what the audience actually sees and hears. Mood is more abstract. Answer choice B best describes the difference between mood and setting.

20. A: Pantomime is an art form that uses gestures and bold facial expressions. It has nothing to do with manipulating objects to make them appear alive. Make-believe is often utilized in the art of puppetry, but it does not always require the use of inanimate objects. Animation occurs onscreen, not onstage, making choice D incorrect. Puppetry is the only art form that involves manipulating inanimate objects to make them look like living beings.

21. B: Professional source materials for both aspiring and practicing educators come in many forms. While visiting libraries, joining theatre organizations, researching, and networking *might* enhance social skills and increase the odds of being included in a community play; these activities do not involve the use of professional source materials. Neither answer choice A nor C is the *best* answer here.

22. C: The first form of theatre originated in ancient Greece. Some experts believe this happened as far back as 500 BC. The Romans developed their own form of theatre shortly after the decline of the Greek government, imitating many aspects of Greek theatre. Medieval theatre, which relied heavily on religious undertones, came next. There are other forms of ancient theatre, but Greek, Roman, and Medieval are the most commonly studied. The English Renaissance is too young to be considered "ancient," as it originated in the 16th century.

23. B: Classical Greek theatre used just three actors onstage, regardless of how many speaking roles there were. They simply went backstage and put on a mask to portray someone new. They did use their voices as powerful performing instruments, making choice A incorrect. Greek theatres were vast in size, accommodating many audience members. It is believed that Asians were the first to incorporate puppetry into theatre performances. Based on this information, answer choices C and D can be eliminated.

24. A: Translated from Italian, *Commedia dell'Arte* means "comedy of craft." It focused on the manner of the performance, not the subject or plot line of a story. Because the Italians were adapting skits from other European countries, they encountered language barriers. For that reason, they started using physical comedy and masks that displayed obvious emotions to reach broader audiences. Scripts were outlined, but not thoroughly written, as performers typically used improvisation to entertain their audience.

25. C: The English Renaissance is commonly known as "the age of Shakespeare." However, William Shakespeare was not the only famous playwright of this time period. Christopher Marlowe, Francis Beaumont, Thomas Middleton, and countless other authors and playwrights emerged on the scene during the English Renaissance. There were also notable comedies and important developments in English music, but this particular time period can best be distinguished by its playwrights.

26. D: This question is best approached by using the process of elimination and asking, "Which of the above answer choices does not belong?" It might also help to think of the word "method" and relate it to the term "methodical," which means organized. If someone is methodical, he is typically patient, has focus, and is a good listener. Therefore, answer choice D is the one that does not belong.

27. A: The teacher in the situation is asking his students to use their sense of smell to assist them during their impromptu performances. When a learning technique involves using sight, smell, touch, hearing, or taste, chances are the teacher is stressing sensory recall. Focus and perception can both be used in the scenario, but neither answer choice is the *best* choice. Characterization really does not apply. Therefore, answer choices B through D are incorrect.

28. C: Practical aesthetics is related to scene breakdown and analysis. It is based on the teachings of Constantin Stanislavski, so answer choice A is incorrect. The Meisner technique was created by Sanford Meisner. It focuses on a series of all-inclusive exercises taught to improve improvisation, so answer choice B can be eliminated. Active analysis, also developed by Stanislavski, is an analytical technique that strengthens an actor's ability to solve problems and take action in the moment. Therefore, answer choice D can also be eliminated.

29. A: Analyzing and studying characters are important aspects of script analysis, but script analysis is much too broad to be the correct choice here. Plot development focuses on the storyline and occurs during the developmental stages before the script is complete. Psychological dissection is not a term that is used in theatre. The question is clearly asking for a choice that is related to better understanding a work's characters and their relationships with one another.

30. C: There are many types of vocal techniques in theater, including warm ups, strengthening exercises, and developmental exercises. It is important to distinguish them from each other. Vocal projection would not be the correct answer here because the teacher is asking her students to *yawn*, not necessarily use their full vocal capacity. Pitch development would require certain musical notes, and breath control would require increments of time. Therefore, answer choice C is the best answer.

31. A: Tempo is related to timing. It is not related to wording, so (B) is incorrect. Phrasing is more closely related to *which* words are sung, not *how* words are sung, so (C) is incorrect. Tone has nothing to do with vowels or mouth shape, just the quality of vocal sound, so (D) is incorrect. Diction is closely related to enunciation. Stressing vowels over consonants is a common vocal exercise used to improve clarity of vocal sound.

32. B: This question can be approached by using the process of elimination. If a performer uses her chest instead of her diaphragm while singing, a lower sound *may* occur, but it is unlikely. Therefore, answer choice A can be eliminated. A higher pitch and a loss of vocal control are both possible when breathing through the chest, but neither answer choice C nor D is the *best* answer. As an educator, it is important to stress *safety first* to students, so answer choice B is the best answer.

33. C: Here is an easy way to remember how to distinguish *pitch* from *tone* using word association. Think of a baseball pitcher. Now think of the *value* the pitcher brings to the team. The pitcher is so valuable that he is awarded Most Valuable Player of the year. *Pitch* is the *value* of a note. Now think of a quality control manager named Tony. Tony also plays the piano. *Tone* measures the *quality* of a note's sound.

34. C: It was Jacques Lecoq, an actor from Paris, who introduced neutral masks into the world of theatre. The term *neutral* has nothing to do with color or material. It simply means "without expression." Lecoq used neutral masks as an actor training tool to create a sense of calm. He wanted his students to understand that while wearing the mask, they cannot be in the past or the future, just in the present. They must be fully aware of themselves and space.

35. D: In order for a student to understand human emotions and characterization, he must be able to recognize facial expressions. Character masks are full masks, each representing a different emotion, such as happy, sad, surprised, mad, etc. Costumes are typically not indicators of emotion, so answer choice A is incorrect. Commedia half-masks display *some* emotion, but their main purpose is to allow for the use of text, so answer choice B is not the best choice. Comedy/tragedy masks are limited in the expressions they can convey, only showing happiness and sadness. Therefore, answer choice C is not the best choice.

36. A: The psychological gesture was developed by the Russian actor and director Michael Chekhov in the early 20th century. His technique was one part physical (before going onstage) and one part visualization (while onstage). It was used when an actor needed to channel the essence of his character. Chekhov did not name the technique after himself, making answer choice D incorrect. Neither character conceptualization nor mental movement are methods related to theatre.

37. A: The operative word in the question is *assumed.* While a director of a production *might* lend a hand to a performer in need of vocal coaching, it is not one of his expected duties. Answer choice A is the one that does not belong. Encouraging cohesion among cast mates, interpreting and approving scripts, and collaborating with crew members are all regularly assumed duties that a successful director must perform.

38. A: According to the scenario in the question, the teacher is passionate about a particular script, but altering the play without permission is illegal, and therefore, not a viable option. Therefore, finding a new script for the seventh graders is the best option, assuming they cannot obtain permission to make alterations. Having the students rewrite the script has a similar issue, but also would be a tedious process and probably not a viable option to achieve with a school group. Leaving the script "as is" is not an option since appropriateness is one of the most important aspects of script selection. If the teacher feels compelled to use this exact script with alterations to specific words, he or she must contact the owner of the rights of the script and request written permission to make alterations, otherwise this is completely inviable.

39. A: By conducting a "chair circle," the director clearly wants to encourage relationships between cast and crew members that are friendly and comfortable. There is no indication that the director wants there to be competition or distinction between the two groups. If that was the case, he would have divided them into separate, opposing teams. Efficiency and productivity will *most likely* increase by conducting activities such as a "chair circle," but the main focus here is on positivity.

40. B: If a director was to give his cast a week off from rehearsals, they might start forgetting lines, or worse, become even more unmotivated. Therefore, answer choice A is not the best choice. Making cast members have dinner together might lower morale and hinder motivation if the cast feels forced, so answer choice C is not the best choice. To choose between answer choices B and D, select the best option. Shortening rehearsals may work, but collectively agreeing on break times promotes collaboration, which can be a powerful motivational device.

41. D: Director placement of an actor onstage could be considered *positioning,* but the technical theatre term is *blocking*. *Staging* is related to set design and prop placement, and has nothing to do with the placement of actors. *Choreography* is related to actor placement onstage, but only when specific dance movements are involved.

42. A: The prices of scripts vary, so it cannot be assumed that purchasing scripts would be less expensive than photocopying them. Therefore, answer choice B can be eliminated. Script pages *can* get lost or shuffled during photocopying, but this is not a good enough reason on its own to purchase scripts *instead* of photocopying them, so answer choice C is incorrect. Sharing scripts is not a good idea because it is inconvenient. Therefore, answer choice D is incorrect.

43. C: Nontraditional casting is when a director gives a role to someone who does not "fit" a particular character description. This is not always related to diversity, and does not always involve giving a role to someone of one race when the character is typically played by someone of another race. For example, a director could give the role of Daddy Warbucks from the stage play *Annie* to a woman and change the character's name to Mama Warbucks. Adverse and curveball casting are not actual theatre terms.

44. C: A theatre is required to pay royalty fees to a playwright any time the play is performed in front of an audience. This includes dress rehearsals or trial runs that are conducted so actors can get a feel for performing in front of others. Often, spectators are not charged an admission. The question of when royalties should be paid has nothing to do with opening night or how much admission is charged, so answer choices A, B, and D are incorrect.

45. D: Blind reading is not used in the theatre industry, so answer choice A can be eliminated. While a cold read is indeed preliminary in nature, answer choice B is incorrect because the technical term is *cold*. Sight-reading is when a performer runs through a piece of sheet music for the first time. It is not related to script reading, so answer choice C is incorrect.

46. B: Experimental theatre is often performed in what is called a black box theatre. This type of theatre can be a converted classroom, an abandoned warehouse, or even an old coffee shop. Usually, there are very few (if any) costs involved with holding performances in a black box theatre. Prosceniums, arenas, and thrusts would be more appropriate for productions that require structured and technical aspects, such as lighting and sound.

47. A: Simply put, a thrust can be described as something that is shoved or *thrust* into an audience from the back wall. Because a thrust is attached to the back wall, audience members can only sit on three sides of the stage. An arena, on the other hand, is typically positioned in the middle of a very large space. Audience members can see a performance from all four sides.

48. B: Answer choice A is incorrect because applying special effects makeup is the responsibility of a makeup designer. Answer choice C is incorrect because incorporating lighting is the responsibility of a lighting designer. Taking care of sound effects is the responsibility of a sound designer. Marketing and increasing ticket sales are the responsibilities of either a house manager or a marketing manager; so, answer choice D is also incorrect. A dramaturg is a person hired to analyze text and research historical facts relevant to a production.

49. B: Theatre gels, also known as *color gels*, are small pieces of film used to change lighting color. Gels have nothing to do with safety, nor are they in actual *gel* form, so answer choice A is incorrect. Sound technicians have no need for color gels, so answer choice C is incorrect. Costume designers would not have a need for color gels, so answer choice D is also incorrect.

50. D: No one other than trained professionals should attempt to fix an electrical cable, especially if sparks are present. Therefore, answer choice A is incorrect. Informing everyone about the potentially dangerous situation may cause panic. Therefore, answer choice B is incorrect. The stage manager or a lighting team member would most likely know how to fix the problem, so calling the fire department may not be necessary. Therefore, answer choice D is a better choice than answer choice C.

51. D: In order to correctly answer this question, one would have to be familiar with specific lighting terminology. Answer choices A through C are not terms that are used in the theatre industry. *Light plot*, though, is a commonly used term. It is a chart or document mapping out precise locations of lights and lighting fixtures. It also lists which color gels will be used and, most importantly, whether they will be used to illuminate, dim, or fade to black.

52. D: Specific lighting refers to a small, controlled area of light. Therefore, answer choice A is incorrect. General lighting involves a much vaster area than specific lighting. An entire stage can be illuminated with general lighting and would obviously involve the use of more than one instrument. Therefore, answer choice B is incorrect. Strip lights are long troughs made of metal that are divided into components. Strip lights do not contain reflectors, so answer choice C is also incorrect.

53. A: A unit set is aptly titled because it consists of separate units that can easily be switched around to change the layout of a set. A unit set is convertible and can take on multiple shapes, but *unit set* is the technical theatre term. Therefore, answer choices B and C are incorrect. The term *uniform* indicates consistency, or something that is constant and not ever-changing. Therefore, answer choice D is incorrect.

54. B: It is vital to always have a first aid kit available to all members involved in a theatre production. Injuries can happen backstage, so a first aid kit should never leave its designated area. Taking it out of its designated area would be a bad idea because someone could injure themselves during the time when the first aid kit was removed. Therefore, answer choices A and C are incorrect. Reporting an injury should be done *after* the kit is returned to its designated area, so answer choice D would not be the next course of action in this situation.

55. B: A flat is a portion of a set, not a *type* of set. Therefore, answer (A) is incorrect. A small piece of scenery that is hinged to another piece of flat scenery is known as a *flipper*, so answer (C) is incorrect. A metal plate that is hinged and used for scenery suspension is called a *flying iron*, so answer (D) is incorrect. A flat is a piece of flat scenery that is framed in wood and usually wrapped in cloth or canvas.

56. A: A painted canvas or backcloth hung at the back of the stage is called a backdrop, so answer choice B is incorrect. A hidden door in the stage where actors can enter and exit is called a *trap*, so answer choice C is incorrect. A piece of cloth used to separate the stage from the audience is called a *curtain* or *grand drape*, so answer choice D is also incorrect.

57. D: Answer choice D is correct because costumes can have many functions onstage. Proper costuming can alter a performer's appearance, distinguish relationships among characters, and convey changes in a character's age *in addition to* deepening the audience's understanding of a character's social status, gender, occupation, and even personality. A costume designer has many important responsibilities. In many cases, he or she can enhance an audience member's experience.

58. C: Similar to a lighting plot, a costume plot is a chart or document created by the designer to inform her team of costuming directions. It lists each costume with accessories, which character will be wearing each costume, and when exactly they will appear onstage. While a costume plot is a *plan* that can be *sketched* or written out like a *script*, the technical term used by professionals in the industry is costume *plot*.

59. D: Theatre costumes can come from anywhere. There is no set standard with respect to how a high school should obtain costuming. Renting costumes can be more cost effective than hiring a seamstress or costume designer to make each wardrobe piece. Donated costumes are obviously even more cost effective than rented ones. Sometimes, when costumes are donated, a seamstress will add accessories to make an old costume or article of clothing more unique or more suitable for a specific performance.

60. A: Theatrical makeup application should start with foundation. All other techniques, such as shading, highlighting, color, and special effects, should go on *after* an even base of foundation is applied to clean skin. Answer choices B and D state that shading and highlighting should be applied before foundation, so both answer choices can be eliminated. Highlighting should be applied to the muscles, and shading should be applied underneath the muscles, so answer choice C is incorrect.

61. A: Physiognomy is the practice of judging a person's character by studying his or her facial features. It is important for a makeup designer to understand physiognomy because people associate character traits with certain facial features. For example, a makeup designer might add frown lines to an actor's face to portray a sad character. A makeup designer might also make an actor's mouth appear fuller than normal because audiences tend to view people with larger mouths as generous.

62. B: The preservatives in theatrical makeup are added to prolong the shelf life of the product. There are no other benefits of preservatives in makeup. They do not prevent the transmission of infection caused by sharing product. The only way to prevent infections is to refrain from sharing makeup. Preservatives will not prevent against color fading, nor will they prevent discoloration under bright theatre lights. Therefore, answer choices A, C, and D are all incorrect.

63. B: A simple prosthetic can be a scar, a wound, or a fake nose. Simple prosthetics are typically made from foam urethane and latex. Scenery backdrops might contain foam or other materials typically found in prosthetics, but latex is not as common a material for scenery backdrops. Costume undergarments are typically made from cloth, so answer choice C is incorrect. Non-slip pads may be constructed out of latex, but they do not contain foam urethane, so choice D is not the best option.

64. D: The director of a theatrical production oversees all artistic endeavors while maintaining astute focus on the performers. However, the director does not handle recording duties. Therefore, answer choice A is incorrect. A crew manager leads backstage efforts, so answer choice B is incorrect. A technical director oversees lighting and sound plots, but would never follow a script to make sure an actor says the correct words. Therefore, answer choice C is not the *best* answer.

65. D: Checking all electrical cables and cord placement so that no one trips over them, practicing backstage procedures in light and dark conditions to familiarize oneself with set up and striking processes, and communicating with other crew members in as few words as possible are all important aspects of backstage etiquette and safety. Striking a set in total darkness, however, is never a good idea. Crew members should always have a flashlight handy.

66. C: Process-centered *drama*, not *theatre*, is a learning technique, not a type of production. Therefore, answer choice A is incorrect. Practical theatre is a term rarely used in the theatre industry today, so answer choice B can be eliminated. Artistic theatre focuses on the actors and the dramatic performance, whereas technical theatre focuses on set construction, sound mixing and recording, light hanging, prop procurement, and all other aspects of theatre that are undetected by the audience.

67. A: Neoclassical theatre was not known for performances with religious undertones. Rather, it was known for its grandiosity, ornate costumes, and melodrama. Therefore, answer choice B is incorrect. Ancient Egyptian theatre did contain religious undertones, but it did not borrow cultural aspects from Medieval theatre, so answer choice C is not the best choice. Indian theatre focused more on rituals and depictions of everyday life, so answer choice D is incorrect.

68. B: *As You Like It* is a comedy by William Shakespeare, so answer choice A is incorrect. *Henry VIII* is considered a historical play, so answer choice C is incorrect. Shakespeare wrote *A Lover's Complaint* as a poem, so answer choice D is also incorrect. Of the answer choices, *Macbeth* is the only Shakespearian play that is considered a tragedy.

69. A: While it would be impossible to memorize every playwright, their works, and where they were from, it is important to memorize a few of the greats. Despite spending a good portion of their writing careers in England, Oscar Wilde and George Bernard Shaw were both born in Ireland. John Millington Synge (*The Playboy of the Western World*) had his plays performed in the famous Abbey Theatre in Dublin, Ireland. Edmond Rostand (*Cyrano de Bergerac*) hailed from France. Anton Chekhov (*The Marriage Proposal* and *The Three Sisters*) was from Russia.

70. C: A farce can be recognized by its outlandish, physical nature. Plots are fast-paced and typically involve improbable circumstances, so answer choice A is incorrect. The term *comedy* is too broad to be the *best* choice here, so answer choice B is incorrect. Slapstick can be identified by exaggerated, sometimes violent gestures, so answer choice D is incorrect. Satire is the best answer because it regularly pokes fun at famous people and/or current events.

71. A: Broadway has impacted society by bringing countless jobs and mass consumerism to the United States, specifically New York. The West End has done the same thing. The West End, however, is in London, England. Therefore, answer choice B is incorrect. Experimental theatre has done little in terms of job creation and mass consumerism, mainly because it appeals to audiences and producers on a budget. Therefore, answer choice C is incorrect. Comedy clubs have created some jobs and generated some consumerism, but their impact is small compared to Broadway. Therefore, answer choice D is not the best choice.

72. C: Paranoia can be related to anxiety, but is more closely linked with delusion, which is rarely associated with performing. Therefore, (A) is incorrect. Claustrophobia is a fear of tight spaces, and has nothing to do with performance, making (B) incorrect. Mood swings can be associated with actors, as actors tend to be dramatic not only onstage, but also in real life. Performance anxiety, however, would be the *best* answer choice for this particular question.

73. A: As it relates to theatre, catharsis is a term that means "to purge the emotions." The terms *purification* and *ablution* have similar connotations, meaning "to cleanse or purify," but neither term is commonly used in the theatre industry. Therefore, answer choices C and D are incorrect. The alienation effect is when a director wants to distance the audience from the characters so they can be observed and critiqued from a non-emotional standpoint. Therefore, answer choice B is incorrect.

74. B: In order to approach this question, one must be able to identify commonly used theatre terms. The only actual theatre term in the answer choices is *alienation effect.* Neither *audience breach* nor *dissection effect* are actual techniques. Someone unfamiliar with theatre terminology, however, may choose one of these answers based on context clues. The third-person effect does exist, but does not relate to the theatre industry. Therefore, answer choices A, C, and D can all be eliminated.

75. A: A good theatre critic adheres to certain guidelines when evaluating productions. These guidelines can typically be categorized under who, what, why, and how. A critic would discuss who acted in the play, what emotions he felt, why the director chose that particular play, and how the technical aspects enhanced the overall feel of the play. The financial impact of a production on a community does not fall under the guidelines commonly followed by theatre critics.

76. D: Because high schools usually do not have the funding available to hire marketers or an advertising firm, students and teachers must be creative. Making posters to display around the school and the community, posting the play's details on the school's website, and sending press releases to the local newspaper are all wonderful ways to promote a production for little to no cost. Therefore, answer choice D is correct.

77. C: Operas and musicals can be sung or performed in any language, so answer choice A is incorrect. There is typically no dancing in operas, whereas there is almost always dancing in musicals, so answer choice B is incorrect. The time between songs can be filled with an orchestra *and* dancing in musicals, so answer choice D is incorrect. The main difference is that operas are usually sung all the way through, while musicals contain spoken dialogue between songs.

78. B: According to the description of the situation, Tim *reflexively* rolled his eyes at Barry, meaning he did what came naturally in the moment. This gave the audience insight into his feelings without Tim having to come out and say it. There is no indication that he followed script directions or was prompted by a vocal cue, so neither answer choice A nor C is correct. Natural impulse is not always implied; it can be quite obvious. Therefore, answer D is not the best choice.

79. B: A teacher must be able to recognize certain traits and abilities in each student in order to guide them toward a successful life path. Self-evaluation would come *after* self-discovery, so answer choice A is not the best choice. To encourage self-discovery is to foster individuality, which is the opposite of conformism, so answer choice D is incorrect. Personal interpretation would call for creativity, not exploration, so answer choice C is incorrect.

80. A: A teacher must encourage creative expression in students, but even more vital is ensuring the physical and mental safety of students. While it is a good idea to take parental warnings into consideration, answer choice B is not the *best* choice. There would be no need to hinder creativity if it became a motivational force for a student, so answer choice C can be eliminated. There would also be no need to thwart creativity if it promoted collaboration among students, so answer choice D is incorrect.

81. D: Conducting open-ended conversations to critique a performance can be a drawn out and unorganized process, especially if students are new to critiquing. Therefore, answer choice A is incorrect. Asking for opinions or instructing students to write down random thoughts would be chaotic approaches to critiquing, so answer choices B and C are not the best choices. Younger students should be introduced to a structured outline that allows them to describe, analyze, interpret, and evaluate others' performances.

82. A: Process-centered drama is most appropriate for very young students who need to learn self-expression, whereas product-centered drama is most appropriate for older students exploring a structured theatre environment. Therefore, answer choice B is incorrect. Students who want to explore the artistic and technical aspects of theatre would likely be too mature for process-centered drama. Therefore, answer choice C is not the best choice. Drama at the K through 12 levels should not be gender specific, so answer choice D is incorrect.

83. C: The operative phrase in the question is *prior experience*. (A) gives no indication that the football player has prior baseball experience, so (A) is incorrect. If a student is known for being shy, and not necessarily her singing skills, she is unlikely to feel comfortable singing in front of the class. Therefore, (B) is incorrect. Given his prior experience with comedy, a class clown would be more likely to take on a comedic role than a serious role. Therefore, (D) is incorrect.

84. A: Bringing electronic gadgetry into a performance, falling asleep, and unwrapping candy with noisy wrappers should be avoided when watching a theatre performance. It is very important to stress these rules of etiquette to students so they will be able to show respect for the actors onstage. If a student did not hear something, it is perfectly acceptable to quietly ask a neighbor for clarification. There are also times when performers interact with audience members, so speaking back would be necessary.

85. B: If Tonya's great-great-grandmother was a historical figure, her portrayal would be based on history *and* heritage. However, Carlos's portrayal of Malcolm X is not based on a current event, so answer choice A is incorrect. There is no indication that Tonya's great-great-grandmother came from a different culture, so answer choice C is not the best choice. Personal experience is typically not relevant during portrayals since portrayals are based on someone else. Therefore, answer choice D is incorrect.

86. A: Partnering students is a great way to promote a better understanding of interpersonal relationships. While problems may arise that need creative problem solving, that is not the focus of the activity, so answer choice B is not the *best* choice. A student may become more confident after being partnered up with another student, but the focus of the activity is on understanding partnerships and relationship building, so answer choice C is incorrect. Exploration of content-related material is not relevant in the scenario, so answer choice D is incorrect.

87. B: By stomping her feet, the actress in the question is communicating her feelings of anger to the audience without using words. Kinetics and gesturing refer to actual body movements, but don't necessarily have to have an emotion attached. Therefore, (A) and (C) are incorrect. Body language relates to positioning and how an individual is feeling internally as opposed to what the person wants to externally communicate to others, so (D) is not the best choice.

88. D: There are many professional development resources available to high school teachers today. One of the best resources to tap into would be other theatre teachers, whether they are in the same school or in another part of the country. Theatre teachers should familiarize themselves with local community actors and conduct research online. An art museum might inspire a lesson plan, but it would be a better professional resource for an art teacher. Therefore, answer choice D is the one that does not belong.

How to Overcome Test Anxiety

Just the thought of taking a test is enough to make most people a little nervous. A test is an important event that can have a long-term impact on your future, so it's important to take it seriously and it's natural to feel anxious about performing well. But just because anxiety is normal, that doesn't mean that it's helpful in test taking, or that you should simply accept it as part of your life. Anxiety can have a variety of effects. These effects can be mild, like making you feel slightly nervous, or severe, like blocking your ability to focus or remember even a simple detail.

If you experience test anxiety—whether severe or mild—it's important to know how to beat it. To discover this, first you need to understand what causes test anxiety.

Causes of Test Anxiety

While we often think of anxiety as an uncontrollable emotional state, it can actually be caused by simple, practical things. One of the most common causes of test anxiety is that a person does not feel adequately prepared for their test. This feeling can be the result of many different issues such as poor study habits or lack of organization, but the most common culprit is time management. Starting to study too late, failing to organize your study time to cover all of the material, or being distracted while you study will mean that you're not well prepared for the test. This may lead to cramming the night before, which will cause you to be physically and mentally exhausted for the test. Poor time management also contributes to feelings of stress, fear, and hopelessness as you realize you are not well prepared but don't know what to do about it.

Other times, test anxiety is not related to your preparation for the test but comes from unresolved fear. This may be a past failure on a test, or poor performance on tests in general. It may come from comparing yourself to others who seem to be performing better or from the stress of living up to expectations. Anxiety may be driven by fears of the future—how failure on this test would affect your educational and career goals. These fears are often completely irrational, but they can still negatively impact your test performance.

Elements of Test Anxiety

As mentioned earlier, test anxiety is considered to be an emotional state, but it has physical and mental components as well. Sometimes you may not even realize that you are suffering from test anxiety until you notice the physical symptoms. These can include trembling hands, rapid heartbeat, sweating, nausea, and tense muscles. Extreme anxiety may lead to fainting or vomiting. Obviously, any of these symptoms can have a negative impact on testing. It is important to recognize them as soon as they begin to occur so that you can address the problem before it damages your performance.

The mental components of test anxiety include trouble focusing and inability to remember learned information. During a test, your mind is on high alert, which can help you recall information and stay focused for an extended period of time. However, anxiety interferes with your mind's natural processes, causing you to blank out, even on the questions you know well. The strain of testing during anxiety makes it difficult to stay focused, especially on a test that may take several hours. Extreme anxiety can take a huge mental toll, making it difficult not only to recall test information but even to understand the test questions or pull your thoughts together.

Effects of Test Anxiety

Test anxiety is like a disease—if left untreated, it will get progressively worse. Anxiety leads to poor performance, and this reinforces the feelings of fear and failure, which in turn lead to poor performances on subsequent tests. It can grow from a mild nervousness to a crippling condition. If allowed to progress, test anxiety can have a big impact on your schooling, and consequently on your future.

Test anxiety can spread to other parts of your life. Anxiety on tests can become anxiety in any stressful situation, and blanking on a test can turn into panicking in a job situation. But fortunately, you don't have to let anxiety rule your testing and determine your grades. There are a number of relatively simple steps you can take to move past anxiety and function normally on a test and in the rest of life.

Physical Steps for Beating Test Anxiety

While test anxiety is a serious problem, the good news is that it can be overcome. It doesn't have to control your ability to think and remember information. While it may take time, you can begin taking steps today to beat anxiety.

Just as your first hint that you may be struggling with anxiety comes from the physical symptoms, the first step to treating it is also physical. Rest is crucial for having a clear, strong mind. If you are tired, it is much easier to give in to anxiety. But if you establish good sleep habits, your body and mind will be ready to perform optimally, without the strain of exhaustion. Additionally, sleeping well helps you to retain information better, so you're more likely to recall the answers when you see the test questions.

Getting good sleep means more than going to bed on time. It's important to allow your brain time to relax. Take study breaks from time to time so it doesn't get overworked, and don't study right before bed. Take time to rest your mind before trying to rest your body, or you may find it difficult to fall asleep.

Along with sleep, other aspects of physical health are important in preparing for a test. Good nutrition is vital for good brain function. Sugary foods and drinks may give a burst of energy but this burst is followed by a crash, both physically and emotionally. Instead, fuel your body with protein and vitamin-rich foods.

Also, drink plenty of water. Dehydration can lead to headaches and exhaustion, especially if your brain is already under stress from the rigors of the test. Particularly if your test is a long one, drink water during the breaks. And if possible, take an energy-boosting snack to eat between sections.

Along with sleep and diet, a third important part of physical health is exercise. Maintaining a steady workout schedule is helpful, but even taking 5-minute study breaks to walk can help get your blood pumping faster and clear your head. Exercise also releases endorphins, which contribute to a positive feeling and can help combat test anxiety.

When you nurture your physical health, you are also contributing to your mental health. If your body is healthy, your mind is much more likely to be healthy as well. So take time to rest, nourish your body with healthy food and water, and get moving as much as possible. Taking these physical steps will make you stronger and more able to take the mental steps necessary to overcome test anxiety.

Mental Steps for Beating Test Anxiety

Working on the mental side of test anxiety can be more challenging, but as with the physical side, there are clear steps you can take to overcome it. As mentioned earlier, test anxiety often stems from lack of preparation, so the obvious solution is to prepare for the test. Effective studying may be the most important weapon you have for beating test anxiety, but you can and should employ several other mental tools to combat fear.

First, boost your confidence by reminding yourself of past success—tests or projects that you aced. If you're putting as much effort into preparing for this test as you did for those, there's no reason you should expect to fail here. Work hard to prepare; then trust your preparation.

Second, surround yourself with encouraging people. It can be helpful to find a study group, but be sure that the people you're around will encourage a positive attitude. If you spend time with others who are anxious or cynical, this will only contribute to your own anxiety. Look for others who are motivated to study hard from a desire to succeed, not from a fear of failure.

Third, reward yourself. A test is physically and mentally tiring, even without anxiety, and it can be helpful to have something to look forward to. Plan an activity following the test, regardless of the outcome, such as going to a movie or getting ice cream.

When you are taking the test, if you find yourself beginning to feel anxious, remind yourself that you know the material. Visualize successfully completing the test. Then take a few deep, relaxing breaths and return to it. Work through the questions carefully but with confidence, knowing that you are capable of succeeding.

Developing a healthy mental approach to test taking will also aid in other areas of life. Test anxiety affects more than just the actual test—it can be damaging to your mental health and even contribute to depression. It's important to beat test anxiety before it becomes a problem for more than testing.

Study Strategy

Being prepared for the test is necessary to combat anxiety, but what does being prepared look like? You may study for hours on end and still not feel prepared. What you need is a strategy for test prep. The next few pages outline our recommended steps to help you plan out and conquer the challenge of preparation.

Step 1: Scope Out the Test

Learn everything you can about the format (multiple choice, essay, etc.) and what will be on the test. Gather any study materials, course outlines, or sample exams that may be available. Not only will this help you to prepare, but knowing what to expect can help to alleviate test anxiety.

Step 2: Map Out the Material

Look through the textbook or study guide and make note of how many chapters or sections it has. Then divide these over the time you have. For example, if a book has 15 chapters and you have five days to study, you need to cover three chapters each day. Even better, if you have the time, leave an extra day at the end for overall review after you have gone through the material in depth.

If time is limited, you may need to prioritize the material. Look through it and make note of which sections you think you already have a good grasp on, and which need review. While you are studying, skim quickly through the familiar sections and take more time on the challenging parts.

Write out your plan so you don't get lost as you go. Having a written plan also helps you feel more in control of the study, so anxiety is less likely to arise from feeling overwhelmed at the amount to cover.

Step 3: Gather Your Tools

Decide what study method works best for you. Do you prefer to highlight in the book as you study and then go back over the highlighted portions? Or do you type out notes of the important information? Or is it helpful to make flashcards that you can carry with you? Assemble the pens, index cards, highlighters, post-it notes, and any other materials you may need so you won't be distracted by getting up to find things while you study.

If you're having a hard time retaining the information or organizing your notes, experiment with different methods. For example, try color-coding by subject with colored pens, highlighters, or post-it notes. If you learn better by hearing, try recording yourself reading your notes so you can listen while in the car, working out, or simply sitting at your desk. Ask a friend to quiz you from your flashcards, or try teaching someone the material to solidify it in your mind.

Step 4: Create Your Environment

It's important to avoid distractions while you study. This includes both the obvious distractions like visitors and the subtle distractions like an uncomfortable chair (or a too-comfortable couch that makes you want to fall asleep). Set up the best study environment possible: good lighting and a comfortable work area. If background music helps you focus, you may want to turn it on, but otherwise keep the room quiet. If you are using a computer to take notes, be sure you don't have any other windows open, especially applications like social media, games, or anything else that could distract you. Silence your phone and turn off notifications. Be sure to keep water close by so you stay hydrated while you study (but avoid unhealthy drinks and snacks).

Also, take into account the best time of day to study. Are you freshest first thing in the morning? Try to set aside some time then to work through the material. Is your mind clearer in the afternoon or evening? Schedule your study session then. Another method is to study at the same time of day that you will take the test, so that your brain gets used to working on the material at that time and will be ready to focus at test time.

Step 5: Study!

Once you have done all the study preparation, it's time to settle into the actual studying. Sit down, take a few moments to settle your mind so you can focus, and begin to follow your study plan. Don't give in to distractions or let yourself procrastinate. This is your time to prepare so you'll be ready to fearlessly approach the test. Make the most of the time and stay focused.

Of course, you don't want to burn out. If you study too long you may find that you're not retaining the information very well. Take regular study breaks. For example, taking five minutes out of every hour to walk briskly, breathing deeply and swinging your arms, can help your mind stay fresh.

As you get to the end of each chapter or section, it's a good idea to do a quick review. Remind yourself of what you learned and work on any difficult parts. When you feel that you've mastered the material, move on to the next part. At the end of your study session, briefly skim through your notes again.

But while review is helpful, cramming last minute is NOT. If at all possible, work ahead so that you won't need to fit all your study into the last day. Cramming overloads your brain with more information than it can process and retain, and your tired mind may struggle to recall even previously learned information when it is overwhelmed with last-minute study. Also, the urgent nature of cramming and the stress placed on your brain contribute to anxiety. You'll be more likely to go to the test feeling unprepared and having trouble thinking clearly.

So don't cram, and don't stay up late before the test, even just to review your notes at a leisurely pace. Your brain needs rest more than it needs to go over the information again. In fact, plan to finish your studies by noon or early afternoon the day before the test. Give your brain the rest of the day to relax or focus on other things, and get a good night's sleep. Then you will be fresh for the test and better able to recall what you've studied.

Step 6: Take a Practice Test

Many courses offer sample tests, either online or in the study materials. This is an excellent resource to check whether you have mastered the material, as well as to prepare for the test format and environment.

Check the test format ahead of time: the number of questions, the type (multiple choice, free response, etc.), and the time limit. Then create a plan for working through them. For example, if you have 30 minutes to take a 60-question test, your limit is 30 seconds per question. Spend less time on the questions you know well so that you can take more time on the difficult ones.

If you have time to take several practice tests, take the first one open book, with no time limit. Work through the questions at your own pace and make sure you fully understand them. Gradually work up to taking a test under test conditions: sit at a desk with all study materials put away and set a timer. Pace yourself to make sure you finish the test with time to spare and go back to check your answers if you have time.

After each test, check your answers. On the questions you missed, be sure you understand why you missed them. Did you misread the question (tests can use tricky wording)? Did you forget the information? Or was it something you hadn't learned? Go back and study any shaky areas that the practice tests reveal.

Taking these tests not only helps with your grade, but also aids in combating test anxiety. If you're already used to the test conditions, you're less likely to worry about it, and working through tests until you're scoring well gives you a confidence boost. Go through the practice tests until you feel comfortable, and then you can go into the test knowing that you're ready for it.

Test Tips

On test day, you should be confident, knowing that you've prepared well and are ready to answer the questions. But aside from preparation, there are several test day strategies you can employ to maximize your performance.

First, as stated before, get a good night's sleep the night before the test (and for several nights before that, if possible). Go into the test with a fresh, alert mind rather than staying up late to study.

Try not to change too much about your normal routine on the day of the test. It's important to eat a nutritious breakfast, but if you normally don't eat breakfast at all, consider eating just a protein bar. If you're a coffee drinker, go ahead and have your normal coffee. Just make sure you time it so that the caffeine doesn't wear off right in the middle of your test. Avoid sugary beverages, and drink enough water to stay hydrated but not so much that you need a restroom break 10 minutes into the test. If your test isn't first thing in the morning, consider going for a walk or doing a light workout before the test to get your blood flowing.

Allow yourself enough time to get ready, and leave for the test with plenty of time to spare so you won't have the anxiety of scrambling to arrive in time. Another reason to be early is to select a good seat. It's helpful to sit away from doors and windows, which can be distracting. Find a good seat, get out your supplies, and settle your mind before the test begins.

When the test begins, start by going over the instructions carefully, even if you already know what to expect. Make sure you avoid any careless mistakes by following the directions.

Then begin working through the questions, pacing yourself as you've practiced. If you're not sure on an answer, don't spend too much time on it, and don't let it shake your confidence. Either skip it and come back later, or eliminate as many wrong answers as possible and guess among the remaining ones. Don't dwell on these questions as you continue—put them out of your mind and focus on what lies ahead.

Be sure to read all of the answer choices, even if you're sure the first one is the right answer. Sometimes you'll find a better one if you keep reading. But don't second-guess yourself if you do immediately know the answer. Your gut instinct is usually right. Don't let test anxiety rob you of the information you know.

If you have time at the end of the test (and if the test format allows), go back and review your answers. Be cautious about changing any, since your first instinct tends to be correct, but make sure you didn't misread any of the questions or accidentally mark the wrong answer choice. Look over any you skipped and make an educated guess.

At the end, leave the test feeling confident. You've done your best, so don't waste time worrying about your performance or wishing you could change anything. Instead, celebrate the successful completion of this test. And finally, use this test to learn how to deal with anxiety even better next time.

Review Video: Test Anxiety
Visit mometrix.com/academy and enter code: 100340

Important Qualification

Not all anxiety is created equal. If your test anxiety is causing major issues in your life beyond the classroom or testing center, or if you are experiencing troubling physical symptoms related to your anxiety, it may be a sign of a serious physiological or psychological condition. If this sounds like your situation, we strongly encourage you to seek professional help.

Online Resources

Due to our efforts to try to keep this book to a manageable length, we've created a link that will give you access to all of your online resources:

mometrix.com/resources719/nystcetheater166

It's Your Moment, Let's Celebrate It!

Share your story @mometrixtestpreparation